HOW TO RUN A LIMITED COMPANY

H M Williams
Chartered Accountants

How to Run a Limited Company
by Ben Houston, Lisa Sword and Hugh Williams
of H M Williams Chartered Accountants

First published 2010
Reprinted 2011

© 2011 Lawpack Publishing

Lawpack Publishing Limited
76–89 Alscot Road
London SE1 3AW
www.lawpack.co.uk

All rights reserved
Printed in Great Britain

ISBN: 9781906971540
ebook ISBN: 9781907765070

Companies House forms are reproduced with the permission of Companies House.

For convenience (and for no other reason) 'him', 'he' and 'his' have been used throughout and should be read to include 'her', 'she' and 'her'.

Exclusion of Liability and Disclaimer

Contents

Preface

Most books on company law tend to be long and impenetrable. They make it hard for the non-professional company officer to see what he has to do if he wants to (say) hold a meeting, declare a dividend or appoint a new director. In fact, these books make it hard for the professional adviser as well! From our long experience in dealing with such matters – we have had another similar work on company law in print for over 20 years – we know that people who are responsible for ensuring that they keep their company operating within the law want a simple guidebook on what to do.

This is what this book sets out to do. Nowhere does it adopt this philosophy more than at the very end where we have included some pages of 'quick cribs', so that if you have carried out a particular function some years ago and just need to be reminded what needs to be done, you should find the answer very speedily there. That said, the whole book is meant to help you get to what you want to know with the minimum of delay and we naturally hope you will find it helpful.

If you have any comments on how this book might be improved, please let us know.

Ben Houston, Lisa Sword and Hugh Williams

H M Williams Chartered Accountants
53 Valley Road
Plympton
Devon
PL7 1RF

mail@hmwilliams.co.uk

01752 334950

A word of warning for those familiar with the statutory administration of limited companies

Since 1 October 2009 there has been a sea-change in the way companies are formed and constituted. It might be helpful if we summarise the changes:

All of the familiar forms for filing at Companies House have changed. Old forms are no longer being accepted after 30 September 2009 and there are many new forms for procedures where, in the past, one used a more generic form, or generic form of wording.

The new Annual Return form is much longer.

The Memorandum is now an extremely short document – see sample enclosed.

The Standard Articles for small companies used to be known as Table A. Standard Articles will still be available but they are now known as Model Articles and can be found in Statutory Instrument 2008 No 3229.

There is no longer a term 'authorised share capital', but companies may opt to keep it. This means that directors can issue shares at their discretion, unless the company passes resolutions that impose restrictions.

You can now have a Single Member PLC.

Companies now have the power to state in their Articles what percentage of votes is required for certain changes.

Meetings may be conducted by phone, teleconferencing or email – or not at all.

A director can be resigned from office if he has been absent without permission from all directors' meetings for six months.

The new form for incorporation IN01 is much more detailed than the forms it replaces. Electronic incorporation is expected to become the norm to cater for all this detail.

Statutory registers need only be kept for ten years.

There will be a new register of directors' residential addresses.

Accounts will have to be filed at Companies House one month earlier than hitherto – it is now normally nine months after the end of the financial year instead of ten.

Please be particularly warned that, as we say on page 54, the penalties for the late filing of company accounts have increased dramatically. Please make sure you file on time.

If you become a PROOF customer (the Registrar's PROtected Online Filing scheme), this should protect your company becoming a victim to corporate identity fraud.

As we have said, all this (and there's a lot more besides) marks a veritable sea-change in the way companies are administered. It is proving quite a headache for all involved in company administration and all we can say as we write in anticipation of what is likely to become a chaos as the new rules are implemented is 'Good luck!'.

This book is dedicated to Gail

CHAPTER 1

Introduction

What is a limited company?

A limited company is a legal entity, separate from any individual involved. It is run by individuals who have specific responsibilities but it owns its own assets; it is liable for its own debts and those who use and run limited companies must always remember that, for example, the money in a company's bank account belongs to the company and not to the directors, nor to the shareholders.

Being a separate legal entity means that it must be run according to set rules and the government department primarily responsible for ensuring that a company adheres to those rules is Companies House.

Companies House, as we will see later, is a highly efficient organisation in Cardiff and, whenever help is needed with company administration, it is highly likely that you will find a prompt answer by calling it on 0303 1234 500.

What types of limited company are there?

There are seven types of limited company:

1. **Private companies**

    These are used mainly by small businesses and the way they need to be managed within company law is the main purpose of this book.

2. **Public companies**

    These are used by larger businesses and, while they share a great number of the same secretarial procedures as private companies, we do not spend long in this book dealing with public companies.

3. Companies Limited by Guarantee

This type of company has no share capital. Companies limited by guarantee are used mainly by charities and the way they are run is substantially the same as for private companies. The member's liability is limited to an amount the member has personally guaranteed to contribute to the assets of the company if it is wound up; this guarantee also applies for a period of one year after membership has ceased. As we go to press there are plans to introduce a new type of charitable structure called a Charitable Incorporated Organisation (CIO), which will report to the Charity Commission, not to Companies House. We understand that it will be easy for companies limited by guarantee to be converted into a CIO and plan to produce a book on their administration in the near future.

4. European Public Companies (EPCs)

These may be useful for businesses operating in more than one EU member state. They may form part of a European Interest Grouping (EIG) but, as with EPCs, we do not deal with EIGs in this book.

5. Overseas companies

These companies are, somewhat obviously, not registered in the UK and cannot be dealt with in this book.

6. Unlimited companies

These are like normal companies but the members' liability is not limited. They do not have to file accounts at Companies House and they can be converted to limited and vice versa. Unlimited companies are relatively rare so they are not dealt with in this book.

7. Community Interest Companies (CICs)

These were started in 2004 to allow socially minded entrepreneurs to make profits for good causes. They pay tax, file accounts at Companies House but they cannot be a charity and so they cover a relatively rare sector and we do not deal with them in this book. The key thing to remember when preparing accounts for CICs is to give a very full description of the company's activities. There is a great deal of helpful information about these on the Companies House website: www.companieshouse.gov.uk.

In addition to the above there are also:

8. Limited Liability Partnerships (LLPs)

These are not companies as such but, for the purposes of administration, they have to follow broadly similar rules to those for private companies. As with unlimited companies we include reference to some of the LLP forms in this book.

9. **Right to Manage Companies (RTMs) and Commonhold Associations (CAs)**

   Both of these were introduced in 2002 but they are all limited by guarantee and so please regard them all as such.

10. **Single Member Companies**

    These are private companies that have just one shareholder. They are treated the same as all private companies. Companies limited by guarantee can also be Single Member Companies.

This book concentrates on the administration of private companies, although much of what follows will be applicable to some, if not all, of the other types.

When should I use a limited company?

As accountants we are often asked this question and we usually say that it all depends.

Most people when setting out in business shouldn't think of forming a limited company. If you ask the people at Companies House, they will tell you that far too many companies are formed each year and either they are not even used and remain dormant, or those who run them find themselves in a jam (often of a tax nature) that would never have happened if they had traded as a sole trader or partnership.

In principle, most people should start in business on their own as a sole trader or in partnership with others. If the profits are small, they would pay less tax and enjoy less hassle and lower professional fees than if they trade through a limited company.

Again in principle, limited companies can be useful when profits approach £100,000 and especially when the proprietors do not wish to draw all of the profits out for their own personal use.

Another instance where incorporation might be sensible is if a number of individuals wish to go into business together and wish to take advantage of limited liability.

A further instance would be where someone wants to set up a business with a view to growing it and selling it. A limited company is easier to sell than, for example, a partnership, because, with a limited liability company, the whole business comes as a complete package and the accounts are more reliable from the purchaser's point of view.

As accountants we nearly always advise our clients to start off as sole traders and then incorporate at a later stage if and when the timing is right and the tax savings become more advantageous and appropriate.

In summary, the advantages of a company are:

1. Limited liability. In theory and in law the shareholders are not personally liable for the debts of the company. The company can only ask shareholders to pay for their shares in full, if they have not already done so. The shareholder's responsibility is limited to this amount and this amount is determined when the shareholder agrees to buy shares. Should the business fail, the creditors cannot obtain possession of shareholders' assets, such as homes or cars, in settlement of debts. However, the directors may find themselves liable to pay the company's debts. Limited liability is the main reason why so many businesses are incorporated.

2. Capital can be raised with relative ease because investors can buy shares in the company. This does not mean, however, that a new company can simply offer shares to the general public. Share offers are regulated by law.

3. Subject to the Articles of Association, shares can be transferred to existing members and to family members as gifts or otherwise. It is possible to sell your shares to other people, but not in a general offer to the public. Investors in a private company do not receive the same protection as they would have if they were investing in companies listed on the Stock Exchange.

4. Since the company is an independent legal entity, it does not cease to exist because one of the shareholders dies or retires. It is therefore easier to ensure the continuity of a company rather than of a partnership.

The disadvantages of a company are:

1. It must comply with statutory rules and disclose information to the public.

2. It is usually the most expensive form of business to organise and run, although a partnership can be equally expensive, especially a Limited Liability Partnership.

3. Both the company and the individual shareholders and directors have to make Tax Returns.

4. Record-keeping (such as keeping a minute book) can be more extensive for a company.

5. Winding up a company and in many cases even changing its structure can be more complicated and expensive than for partnerships and sole traders.

6. Please remember it's not your money. Any money in the company's bank account belongs to the company and it can only be taken out as a dividend or wage, or set against money you put into the business.

Should I form a private or a public company?

A *public* company is defined as one where:

- It must have two directors, one of whom must be an individual; the other can be a corporate director.

- It has been registered with Companies House as such.

- Its name ends '...Public Limited Company' or 'PLC'.

- It must have a company secretary, who must be qualified in one or more ways.

- It cannot start in business until it has been issued with a trading certificate. To do this it must deliver form SH50 to Companies House.

- It can be re-registered as a private company by submitting form RR06.

- The Memorandum of Association states it to be public.

- It has an issued share capital of not less than £50,000.

All other companies are private companies.

A private company has the following features or advantages:

- Only one shareholder is required.

- Only one director is required. If there is only one director, he must be a real person and not another company. As a firm of chartered accountants we advise the appointment of at least more than one shareholder or director because, if a single shareholder/director dies, who is there to administer the company and decide its future?

- The shareholder(s) and director(s) may be the same person. If this is the case, then all resolutions must be in writing.

- A private company does not require a trading certificate.

- There are no minimal capital requirements.

- The hassle surrounding private companies is generally less than that surrounding public companies.

A private company may be converted into a public company and vice versa.

CHAPTER 2

Company formation

How do I form a limited company?

To form, or incorporate, a company you need to send the following documents to Companies House:

- Form IN01 (available from the Companies House website www.companieshouse.gov.uk).

- The completed Memorandum of Association (see sample in Appendix 2).

- The company's constitution (known as its 'Articles of Association') unless you decide to adopt the Model Articles (see Appendix 2.2). In this case you do not need to submit the company's proposed Articles and you mark form IN01 accordingly.

You can submit the forms either by post or electronically.

Electronic incorporation

As mentioned, you can form a company by post (with aid of guidance notes GP1 from the Companies House website) but it is now far more common for companies to be created using the internet. There are two main ways to do this:

1. New company electronic incorporations

If you want a brand new company tailored to your circumstances (and this is what most people want), you need to approach a company formation agent offering this type of service. It is not only the most popular form of incorporation, but also the fastest (in most cases same day incorporation). It is now recognised as the most convenient way to create a company.

If this sounds like what you would like to do, type 'electronic incorporation' into any recognised search engine and tens of company formation agents offering this service will appear. If you are unsure which company to use, you could ask your accountant or visit the Companies House website as it has some recommendations.

A few things to note for electronic incorporation are:

- Directors and secretaries will need to provide extra information for security purposes, such as various letters or numbers of the following: eye colour, National Insurance number, father's first name, town of birth, passport number and home phone number.

- Most formation agents have safeguards in place to make sure the company is accepted first time.

- If you were to incorporate online, there are various packages that can be bought depending on your needs. Generally, the cheapest package that can be bought is just for companies that will be left dormant; the medium package will suit most people's needs. The most expensive package usually includes paper copies of the Articles of Association and an incorporation certificate sent to you by post.

- With the cheaper options you may not get a proper incorporation certificate; you will receive an electronic version which will have to be printed off onto a certain quality paper.

2. Off-the-shelf companies

This way is less common than the above and therefore more for your information. Off-the-shelf companies are companies that have already been incorporated but currently lie dormant and have never traded. These will then be sold to a member of the public for a set fee, usually along with the forms to change the company name, directors, secretary, year end, share ownership and registered office.

I want to form a limited company but it all seems so daunting. Who can I get to help me with all this?

We would suggest that you ask a firm of chartered accountants to deal with it for you but make sure that they quote for the work before they begin so you know what it will all cost and what they are going to do for you.

Before you instruct someone else to form your company for you, you should look at our suggested pre-incorporation checklist in Appendix 1.1 where we list all of the things you should have sorted out in your mind before giving instructions. This will save time and it might also save you fees.

What do I need to have decided before forming a limited company?

These are the following matters that should have been decided before instructing whoever it is that is going to form the company. They are broadly similar to the pre-incorporation checklist in Appendix 1.1, namely:

- The company name.
- What the company is going to do.
- Who will be the shareholders?
- How much money or other assets will each shareholder invest?
- Are all the shareholders to have the same class of shares or will there be different classes?
- If there are to be different classes, what are they to be? (If this sounds confusing, then don't worry; most companies are formed with say 100 ordinary shares and the shareholders involved decide how many shares each is to hold.)
- Who are the directors going to be?
- Who is the managing director going to be? You don't have to have a managing director.
- The accounting year end.
- Where will the registered office be situated? This is usually the same as the place of business.

Having listed the above essential matters it is also extremely prudent for those who are to join together in business to discuss and decide the following practical matters, which we call an Investors' Aspiration Form (see Appendix 1.2):

Each person should openly declare:

- What he hopes this business will achieve.
- Why he thinks this business will be successful.
- What he will bring to the business.
- How much time he will devote to the business.
- What he would like to do in the business.
- What he does not want to do in the business.
- Who will be the business' boss.
- Whether he will be prepared to bring more money to the business should it be necessary to do so.

- When he would like to retire from the business.

- What he hopes to earn from the business each year.

- What dividends he would hope to be paid.

- What benefits he would like the business to provide, for example, a car, mobile phone, etc.

- What he would like to happen to his shares in the event of his early death.

- Who should sign cheques, etc.

- Over what level of payment should a cheque have more than one signature.

- Where the business should bank.

- Whether accounts should be prepared more frequently than annually.

- Which firm of accountants should be appointed.

- Whether there should be a shareholders' agreement

We have included this list as a suggested procedure for you to consider and we further recommend that you copy the pages from Appendix 1.2 and get all of those who will be working with you in the company to fill in his own copy, get someone knowledgeable and independent such as your accountant to review them and say if he thinks your replies indicate whether you are going to work together well and are likely to get on and agree on how to run the business.

Shareholders' agreement

It is usually prudent to have a shareholders' agreement prepared by a solicitor. In case you don't know what a shareholders' agreement is, or its purpose, it is the equivalent of a partnership agreement in the case of a partnership. A shareholders' agreement sets out how the shareholders have agreed to work together. We provide a list of the main headings to be found in a typical shareholders' agreement in Appendix 1.3.

Once this formal legal document is signed, it formalises the relationship of the shareholders and, in effect, makes legally binding those aspects that we suggest all participators declare on their 'aspiration form'.

What do I have to do in connection with the business name?

First of all there are two types of name you need to be aware of: the company name and the business name, or trading name.

The company name is the formal name of the company and it will be registered at Companies House under that name. The business or trading name is the name under which you wish your company to trade and this may or may not be the same as the company name. In case you are unsure what this paragraph actually means, the company name of the company that has published this book is 'Lawpack Publishing Ltd', although, if you visit their website you will tend to see just their business or trading name of 'Lawpack'. In this case the trading name is similar to the company name but the same would apply if Lawpack were to refer to its products as being published by a completely different name such as 'Helpful Books' or something similar.

The registrar of companies (Companies House) is more concerned with company names than business or trading names because the company name is the one that will appear on all of its records and forms; nonetheless, neither the company name nor the business name may infringe the rules regarding company names, which can be found in its booklets available from the Companies House website under 'guidance notes'.

The first thing you need to ensure after you have selected a name for your company is that the name does not already exist. You can check this by looking at your local telephone directory, doing a search on the internet or, above all, going to the Companies House website and seeing if your choice is already being used. Go to www.companieshouse.gov.uk, select 'WebCHeck' and type in the name you want. Select 'Company Name Availability Search'; this will give you prior notification if your preferred name will be rejected.

Your choice of name will have to be approved by Companies House before your company can be registered and this means that, apart from avoiding a name that is already in use, you must also avoid using certain sensitive words and names that you will find listed in the above-mentioned booklets. For example, words such as 'British' and 'Royal' are highly unlikely to be accepted.

If in any doubt, one way to proceed would be to submit the name to Companies House and see whether it's acceptable.

If you are simply, and always, going to trade under the full company name, then all you need do is display that name formally, accurately and clearly at all of your places of business. This is not only a legal requirement but also only common sense to tell your customers, etc. that that is your place of business. In other words, if you display your full name clearly on the outside of your business premises, that will suffice for this particular legal requirement. Otherwise ensure that the name of your company is clearly displayed on the front door of your business premises.

While doing this, if appropriate, you should also display another form stating that that place is the situation of the registered office of your business. We show you how to do this in Appendix 1.4a and 1.4b.

If you are going to trade under a different business name, then you should display the Notice of Particulars of Ownership form, as shown in Appendix 1.4a, in the reception or equivalent area of your business premises. The particular layout of this form does not have to be used; you can prepare your own form but it must use this precise wording.

If the registered office of your company is not at your own trading address (e.g. you might decide to ask your accountants if they will be the place of your registered office), then, while you would not have to display the notice stating the situation of the registered office – that would have to be done by your accountants – you would still have to display the Notice of Particulars of Ownership form if you are trading under a separate business name that's not the same as the name registered at Companies House.

If you have a company name that you wish to protect, then, by registering it at Companies House, you can be sure nobody else will use it. You may also wish to have the comfort of protecting it as a trademark with the Intellectual Property Office, see www.ipo.gov.uk.

You should be aware that there is no longer a separate register of business (trading) names.

Once you have decided on a definite name then it (together with the word 'limited') must appear on all your stationery, emails, advertising, websites, etc.

If you have bought a company and want to change its name, please see Appendix 3.1 for how to do that.

When a limited company is formed, what happens and what forms do I need to deal with?

Certificate of Incorporation

Before we describe what you should do with this form, it might be more sensible if we start by suggesting that you set up a special ring-bound file, which might be called 'Your Company Name – Statutory Books' because once you have set this up with ten divider tabs (and we show you a suggested contents sheet for this file in Appendix 1.29) the rest of the items in this section can be easily filed away.

The Certificate of Incorporation sent by Companies House (and we show you an example in Appendix 2.4) is the legal proof that your company exists and is free to start trading. This should be filed under Tab 1 of your folder.

Memorandum and Articles – what are they?

The Memorandum and Articles have changed considerably as a result of the 2006 Companies Act; indeed, the Memorandum is a shadow of its former self.

The Memorandum is now extremely short and simple and we give you an example in Appendix 2.1.

The Articles can be more or less anything you want, so long as they abide by the law; however, the most sensible thing to do is to use the Standard Articles that the government has provided for this purpose. They used to be called Table A, but are now known as Model Articles. We include a copy of these in Appendix 2.2 and under normal circumstances we suggest that new companies adopt these Articles. They are free and, being Model Articles, do not have to be registered at Companies House.

However, do be aware that Model Articles do not allow your company to have features such as:

- partly paid shares – your shares must be paid in full;
- different classes of shares – you can only have one class;
- alternate directors – see chapter 3.

If you want any of these and some other features to be available to your company, then you can form the company with the Model Articles, but you will have to amend them as per Appendix 3.2.

In other words you can use one of three types of Articles:

1. Model Articles
2. Amended Model Articles
3. Bespoke Articles

There are three variations of the Model Articles available:

1. Suitable for private companies
2. Suitable for companies limited by guarantee
3. Suitable for public limited companies

The statutory books

The statutory books are official records of the company that hardly anyone ever sees; so if you have not heard of them, don't be too downhearted.

They are the records of the names and addresses of the shareholders plus details of their holdings, the details of the directors, the details of the company secretary, if one has been appointed, plus a number of other records which should be kept either on paper, in a book or electronically.

We give suggested layouts for these records under 'suggested procedures' and, because we recommend that the records, whether kept electronically or not, should be kept in hard copy form as well, we suggest that they are filed in an A4 ring-binder with ten divider cards that we have mentioned. If you keep all the statutory books in one of these, it would be as well to use our suggested contents sheet at the front so you know what's in the file and where to find it.

The statutory books should be kept at the company's registered office, but if you want to change their location then file form AD02 or AD03 or possibly AD04.

All of the statutory books, with the exception of the directors' private addresses, should be available for inspection by members and indeed by anyone else, free of charge.

What do I have to do once the company has been formed?

When a company has been formed you will find that you are sent an incorporation certificate. Our first suggestion is that you start an A4 ring-binder which you call your company's statutory books. The Certificate of Incorporation will be filed under Tab 1.

You will also have (or have to create using the template in this book – see Appendix 1) the following registers:

- Register of shareholders
- Register of directors
- Register of secretaries (if you appoint one)
- Register of charges (if your company is taking out a mortgage)
- Register of debenture holders (if there are to be any)
- Register of directors' residential addresses (which is not to be made public)
- Register of seals (if you are going to use a seal)

You should then:

- Issue the share certificates.
- Display the company's registered name (see above).
- Display the company's business or trading name if that is not the same as the registered name (see above).
- Write to your suppliers and customers advising them of the change in status, if your business has been a sole trader or partnership and you have incorporated it.
- Hold the first board meeting to consider matters such as:
  - appointing additional directors (chapter 3);
  - appointing a chairman/managing director;
  - appointing a secretary (chapter 4);
  - appointing auditors/accountants (chapter 13);
  - changing accounting reference date (chapter 12);
  - whether or not to use a seal (chapter 8).

- Inform the tax, PAYE and VAT authorities.

- Open a bank account (if applicable). You will not be able to continue trading using a bank account that had been used by a sole trader or partnership. One of the first activities will be the banking of the money that has been invested in the company's shares.

- Create the company's stationery (chapter 14).

- Put a suitable signature into your email system.

CHAPTER 3

Directors

What are directors?

Directors are the people charged with running the company. They are the company's managers, if you like. It is on their shoulders that the responsibility for what the company does, rests. Directors may also be shareholders.

Directors have specific responsibilities which may be summarised as follows:

- Their prime responsibility is to the company itself.

- They must act within the powers conferred on them by company law and the company's own constitution.

- They must promote the success of the company.

- They must exercise independent judgement.

- They must exercise reasonable care, skill and diligence.

- They must avoid conflicts of interest and must not use their position to further their own interests.

- They must ensure that the company is able to pay its debts and may be held personally liable if it is unable to do so.

- They are responsible for ensuring that the company files all of the requisite forms at Companies House, including the annual statutory accounts.

- In principle, they must not accept personal benefits from third parties.

- They must declare any personal interest in a proposed transaction.

A director's status and duties

A director is an agent and an officer of the company.

A director need not necessarily hold shares in the company, unless the Articles say that he should.

Can a director also be company secretary?

Yes he may but, if he is the sole director he may not also be company secretary. That said it is no longer a requirement to appoint a company secretary.

Is there a minimum number of directors?

Every company must have at least one natural (i.e. human) director. What this means is that a company may not have a sole corporate director.

The law says that you should have at least one director but, if your company operated under Table A (and many did and still do) that says that there should be a minimum of two directors. If your company was formed before 1 October 2009 and if you want to have just one director, then you must change your Articles – see Appendix 3.2.

Is there a minimum age for being a director?

Yes, it's 16. Anyone under 16 who is holding office after 1 October 2008 will automatically cease to hold office.

Is there a maximum age for being a director?

No.

How do I appoint a director?

The first directors are appointed on form IN01.

The board may appoint additional directors and their details must be submitted to Companies House on form AP01 within 14 days of the appointment. Such additional appointments must also be written up in the register of directors.

The suggested procedure is shown in Appendices 1.31 and 3.4.

Do directors have to retire by rotation?

In the past, directors were normally appointed for three-year periods and at both the next Annual General Meeting (AGM) after their appointment and at the end of each successive third year of service they had to offer themselves for re-election at the following Annual General Meeting. This requirement has now been dispensed with.

However, if you continue to hold Annual General Meetings, you may need to check with your Articles whether the retirement is still required under the company's own internal rules. It is no longer a requirement of company law.

Does a director need a service contract?

As an employee a director must be given a contract of employment, along with all other employees. However, if he needs a separate employment contract drawn up, this will be called a director's service contract.

Who actually is a director?

In principle this must seem a silly question. Surely the directors are those people who have been formally appointed?

Well, indeed this is the case but other people, by virtue of the role they perform in the business may be deemed to have become shadow directors and, even though they have not been formally appointed, by virtue of their behaviour they could find themselves liable for punishment along with the formal directors in the case of the company failing.

How can a director retire or resign?

A director may resign by notifying the company in writing or orally. To do so he should write to the board along the lines suggested in Appendix 1.32.

How can a director be dismissed?

A director may be removed from office by ordinary resolution of the shareholders passed at a general meeting. Special notice must be given and the director has the right to make representations at the meeting. He can also make written representations before the meeting which must either be circulated to all members before the meeting or read out at the meeting.

In addition, a director can be resigned from office if he has been absent without permission from all directors' meetings for six months.

Both of these methods should be used as a last resort because less blood tends to be spilt if a director can be persuaded to resign; and do bear in mind that a director is entitled to sue for breach of contract.

Also please remember to file form TM01(see Appendix 4) within 14 days of the termination.

Can a director get compensation for loss of office?

Compensation for loss of office may only be paid if it is approved by an ordinary resolution passed by members at a General Meeting, or if it is authorised in the director's service contract.

Can directors be disqualified for failing to deliver documents to Companies House?

Yes. They can be disqualified from being a director and from acting as one for up to five years if they fail to deliver the required Companies Act forms and other statutory documents on time.

What sort of director are there?

Managing directors

A managing director may be appointed but his responsibilities do not make him automatically more liable for a company's failure than the rest of the board. If he is given any additional powers, they must be formally delegated to him by the board.

Chairman

The duty of a chairman is to chair company and board meetings. He would normally be the managing director but the directors may appoint any of their number to chair a board or shareholders' meeting. Under the Model Articles, a chairman is entitled to a casting vote. The normal procedure when using a casting vote is to vote for the status quo ante. This means that a casting vote should be used to keep options open rather than steamroller resolutions through.

We give some more details on a chairman's duties in chapter 10.

Executive directors

These are directors who have a job to do at the company, in addition to attending board and other meetings.

Non-executive directors

These are directors who do not have a job to do at the company, and their duties tend to be limited to the attendance of board and other meetings. Non-executives will not be held any less liable for a company's failure. Under the law they are expected to be as well informed about the position of the company as executive directors. They can never hide behind the excuse that they never knew what was going on.

Shadow directors

These, as we have said, are those who, by their actions, hold themselves out to be directors, even though they have not been formally appointed. Such a person could be a major shareholder or someone whose business card describes him as a sales director but who has not been formally appointed as a director. Such people could well be held as liable as the rest of the board if a company fails.

Alternate directors

Alternate directors are people appointed by directors to act in their place, for example, when they are unable to attend a board meeting. The directors will have to give their consent that this person be appointed. Alternate directors are responsible for their own actions in addition to acting as an agent of the director who appoints him.

Directors as shareholders

Unless the Articles state otherwise, a director is not obliged to buy shares in a company.

Can a director be lent money by a company?

This may surprise you, because the answer is 'yes' under certain circumstances, such as the members approving the arrangements by ordinary resolution.

Approval by the board is not required for personal purposes up to £10,000, nor for directors' expenses up to £50,000, nor for legitimate legal fees and also not if the company's normal business is that of money lending. Please be aware that there are likely to be adverse tax consequences if money is lent to a director. Also, it must be properly and fully disclosed in the accounts.

CHAPTER 4

Company secretary

What is a company secretary?

The company secretary, where one has been appointed, is the individual charged with ensuring that the company fulfils all of its statutory duties – see below.

It should be noted that, while it is not essential for a company secretary to be appointed, it is essential that the duties mentioned below are fulfilled and so, in our view, it is prudent to appoint someone specifically to attend to these matters and it would seem sensible to appoint that person as the company secretary. If this is not done, there is a danger that some duties will not be done.

In addition, if the company's Articles provide for it to have a secretary, then it must appoint one.

What are his duties?

While the following is not an exhaustive list of the duties a company secretary would be expected to attend to, if the company secretary ensures that all of them have indeed been attended to, it's unlikely that he will have been failing in his duty. The company secretary must:

- Assist the chairman with the corporate governance of the company.

- Deal with all the duties necessary when a company is newly formed (see chapter 2).

- Send notice of the Annual General Meeting (AGM), if one is to be held, and all general meetings to the members.

- Send a copy of the statutory accounts to the members.

- Send a notice of all general meetings to the company auditor, if one has been appointed.

- Keep the minutes of general (i.e. members') meetings.

- Attend to dividend payments.

- File accounts and the Annual Return at Companies House and in good time.

- Keep the statutory books (e.g. registers of members, directors, etc.) up to date.

- Notify changes of secretary and directors to Companies House.

- Ensure that the company stationery, email signatures and display signs and boards show all the details, etc. that the law requires.

- Send notices of board meetings to the directors.

- Keep the minutes of board meetings.

- Ensure that the necessary insurance certificate, registered office details and health and safety notices are properly displayed in places of work.

- Keep the Certificate of Incorporation in a safe place.

- Ensure that changes caused by death, bankruptcy or change of name (e.g. on marriage) are duly entered in the statutory registers.

- Pay Stamp Duty when necessary.

- In the case of a private company, ensure that shares are not offered to the public.

We hope the suggested procedures in Appendices 1 and 3 will help anyone who acts as a company secretary fulfil most, if not all, of his duties.

How is he appointed?

If you decide to appoint a company secretary when the company is incorporated, his details are included on form IN01 and is appointed this way.

If you wish to appoint a company secretary subsequent to incorporation, then you will need to submit form AP03.

Who may be appointed?

It is common for a limited company to appoint one of its directors, or a senior employee, as company secretary but to get the firm's accountants to actually do the work. If this happens, then, while he must be very diligent if this is all he does, all the company secretary would then have to do is 'sign on the dotted line' those forms, etc. which the professionals have prepared. However, while private companies do not have to appoint a qualified company secretary, because such people will always be in danger of being regarded as directors or shadow directors, we suggest the following people are not appointed as company secretary:

- Anyone under the age of 16.

- Anyone disqualified from being a company director.

- An undischarged bankrupt, unless he has been given permission by the court.

The company's auditor may not be appointed company secretary.

How is he removed?

A secretary can be removed by a resolution of the directors. A secretary can be disciplined, dismissed or resign in the same manner as any other employee subject to the terms of his contract.

If you employ someone outside the company to be the company secretary, his removal, etc. will be subject to any relevant contract or agreement.

How does he resign?

A secretary may resign by submitting his resignation in writing to the board, who may or may not decide to replace him. If he is not replaced, then form TM02 should be filed. If he is replaced, then form AP03 will also have to be submitted (see Appendix 4).

Please see Appendix 1.33 for suggested procedures to follow.

What is his status?

The secretary's status is not precisely defined in law. He used to be a servant of the company but is now considered to be its chief administrative officer. He therefore has implied authority and, as we say, he could well be regarded as acting as a director, even though he has not been formally appointed as such.

CHAPTER 5

Registered office

It is compulsory for a limited company to have a registered office at all times, although this address need not be the place at which the company conducts its business. The address of the registered office cannot be a PO Box and it should be a place where someone can deal with correspondence that is sent to the company.

The intended situation of the registered office will be stated on form IN01 but it is possible to change this address. If it is changed, it cannot be changed away from the country in which it has been incorporated.

If you want to change the registered office you should use form AD01 and file it within 14 days of the decision being taken. The change will only take effect when the form has been registered at Companies House.

When a registered office is changed, Companies House verify this with Royal Mail.

The company's name must be clearly displayed at the registered office by means of a suitable sign. See the suggested procedure in Appendix 1.4.

The situation of the registered office should be clearly shown on all items of business stationery as well as on emails and the company's website.

CHAPTER 6

Annual Return (Form AR01)

Snapshot

An Annual Return is a snapshot of a company's officers, registered office, type of trade, share capital and sometimes shareholders at a certain date. Once submitted, this information will be available for inspection by anyone on the Companies House website.

Deadline and filing fees

The date the return is made up to is normally the date the company was incorporated, so if a company was incorporated on 12 June, unless changed, the Annual Return will always be made up to that date. The maximum period between submitting an Annual Return for a company is one year. The deadline for submission to Companies House is 28 days after the date of the return.

Companies House sends out reminders to the company secretary for each Annual Return required, but it does not now send out paper returns to companies. If you wish to submit the return via post, you can either contact Companies House and request one, or download a sample form from its website. The cost for filing an Annual Return is currently £14 for online submission and £40 for postal submission. (For more information about submitting online, please see chapter 17.)

The Annual Return must be signed by a serving officer of the company.

New for the Companies Act 2006

There is an option not to provide a full list of shareholders for private limited companies on each return every year. However, a complete list must be supplied every three years; it must also be supplied on the company's first Annual Return and if there are any changes in shareholdings in a year without a full list being required, the Annual Return must show the changes.

Another new provision is that, if an officer of the company uses a service address for the statutory register, this must be entered on the Annual Return.

A company is also now not required to show authorised share capital on the Annual Return.

Other information

Companies House uses Standard Industrial Classification (SIC) codes to classify business types. A complete list of these is available on the Companies House website. Sometimes it is difficult to find your exact business type in which case you could either enter a brief description of what the company does or use the closest SIC code(s).

CHAPTER 7

Statutory books

The statutory books are the official records of the company that hardly anyone ever sees; so, as we have already implied, if you have not heard of them, do not be too downhearted. That said, they are very important because they are the very essence of the limited company's formal persona.

They record the names and addresses of the shareholders plus details of their holdings, the details of the directors, the details of the company secretary (if one has been appointed) plus a number of other records, and so they must be kept either on paper, in a book, or electronically.

The most usual statutory books are:

- Register of members.
- Register of directors and secretaries.
- Register of directors' residential addresses, which need not be made public. They can use a service address, such as the address of the registered office, in the register of directors and secretaries.
- Register of share transfers.
- Minute books for directors' meetings as well as shareholders' meetings.
- Accounting records.

Occasionally there needs to be:

- Register of charges (mortgages).
- Register of debenture holders.
- Directors' service contracts.
- Register of applications and allotments – for recording who applies for shares and who is subsequently allotted them – but this is rarely kept nowadays.

All such records need to be kept for ten years.

There is no longer any need to keep a separate register of directors' interests.

We give suggested layouts for these records in Appendix 1.30 and how you fill in the forms should be self-evident. We recommend that the records, whether kept electronically or not, should be kept in hard copy form as well, and suggest that they are filed in an A4 ring-binder with ten divider cards. If you keep them in one of these, it would be as well to have a contents sheet at the front so you know what's in the file and where to find it. We provide a suggested contents sheet for the statutory books in Appendix 1.29.

The statutory books should be kept at the company's registered office but if you want to change their location then file form AD02 or AD03 or possibly AD04 (see Appendix 4).

All of the statutory books should be available for inspection by members (i.e. shareholders) free of charge, and by anyone else, so long as they have a proper purpose in doing so.

The company secretary is responsible for keeping the statutory books up to date.

CHAPTER 8

Company seal

If you have not been supplied with a company seal, then you can ignore this section. In times past, all limited companies were supplied with a company seal and, if you have been provided with one, you can use it as a means of delegating the witnessing of its use to someone other than a director or secretary.

Documents which used to require the impression of the company seal now have to be signed by two directors or by a director and the secretary.

Each time the seal is used it should be noted in the register of seals, a suggested layout for which is included in Appendix 1.30j.

The documents that might be sealed include:

• Issued share certificates

• Deeds

• Contracts

One very seldom sees company seals nowadays and so you are unlikely to need to know about them.

CHAPTER 9

Shares and share capital

What are shares and share certificates?

This is actually rather a good question because, in essence, shares only exist as pieces of paper called share certificates and, as such, have no intrinsic value. What is important is what these pieces of paper represent, which is a share of the ownership of the company. In other words, they are legal documents that will show how much of (how many shares in) a limited company a particular shareholder owns. The total value of shares that have been issued is the 'share capital' of the company.

Shares can be transferred or sold and, so long as the underlying company has a marketable worth, the share certificates are indeed items of value.

What are shareholders?

These are the owners of the shares in a company. They are sometimes called 'members'. They share the ownership of the company and the proportion they own is reflected by the number of shares they hold; hence the term 'shareholder'.

Shareholders don't have any specific responsibilities or duties to perform but, if they fail to attend company meetings and the company fails, in part, even if not in law, it will be the shareholders' fault for non-attendance and for showing no interest.

Shareholders who get rich through doing nothing except banking their twice-yearly dividend cheques, playing no part and showing no interest in what the company is doing, have been the subject of understandable criticism from trade unions and certain political parties. We believe that, wherever possible, shareholders should show an interest in what is going on in the company in which they hold shares and should play an appropriate part by attending meetings. There is no rule that says they have to do this, although there are certain matters that can only be decided by shareholders, for example, changing the company's constitution, changing the share structure and deciding whether or not to wind up the company.

What are the different classes of share?

Ordinary shares

Most shares nowadays are ordinary shares. They carry the greatest risk because if the company fails, holders of these shares get nothing. However, they attract the greatest gain where gain is to be had. Ordinary shares usually carry the right to vote at shareholders' meetings.

Preference shares

Where preference shares have been issued, the holders have the first right to any dividends, although such preferential right is for a fixed dividend. Holders of preference shares rank more highly than any other shareholders in the event that the company is wound up.

Cumulative preference shares

In the case of these shares, if a company is unable to pay a dividend on them in a particular year, the dividend that should have been paid is rolled forward and must be paid in the following year so the holders are entitled to receive both that year's dividend as well as the dividend that has been missed in the previous year.

If a dividend cannot be paid in the following year, both dividends are rolled forward until all cumulative preference dividends have been paid.

The term is really very descriptive and so do not overlook the fact these dividends must be paid before any others. They get preference over all other classes of shares.

Participating preference shares

These are a hybrid between ordinary and preference shares in that they are given preference when it comes to payment of dividends, but they also rank equally with ordinary shares in the event of a winding-up.

Redeemable preference shares

These shares can only be issued if there are no non-redeemable shares (i.e. no other shares) in issue. Professional advice should be sought if you want to issue such shares.

A, B, C shares, etc.

Some ordinary shares are given distinctive letters (such as A, B or C) which can be used for different classes of shareholder in cases where one might wish for the A holders to receive a higher dividend than say the holders of B shares.

Non-voting shares

This means that the holders have no right to vote at meetings.

Debentures

These are loans, not shares, and while debenture holders' details must be kept in a register and they are entitled to receive interest (not dividends) on their loans, they are not members of the company and not entitled to vote at meetings.

Deferred shares

These carry very few rights and are only entitled to repayment in the event of a winding-up.

Nominee shares

These are normal shares (such as ordinary shares) that are held by someone other than the beneficial owner, for example, a trustee or someone holding the shares for someone else. The name of the beneficial owner is not recorded in the shareholders' register.

Where shares are held by nominees a declaration of trust, which will need Stamp Duty of £5 paid on it, must be prepared. We include a standard wording for this under suggested procedures in Appendix 1.18.

What is par value?

Shares are usually called £1 ordinary shares, or 50p ordinary shares, and the given descriptive figure is their 'par value'. This sum does not necessarily reflect the sum paid for the shares and it is highly unlikely to be the same as their current value. You can give your shares any par value you choose, but £1 is the norm.

What is stock?

Stock is another type of share capital and, in nearly every respect, for 'stock' you can read 'shares'. The reason why some companies issue stock is that stock can be divided into any amount you want. For example, while, if you own one share, you can only sell that one share (you cannot sell half of one share), if you own (say) £100 worth of stock you can, if you want, sell two-thirds of your holding or £66.67p worth.

You can no longer convert shares into stock but you can convert stock into shares.

Is there a minimum number of shareholders?

The minimum number of shareholders for a private or public company is one.

What are authorised shares and issued shares?

Authorised shares are no longer required, although many companies continue to use the term. What this term refers to is the number of shares that the company is entitled to issue, but it is not necessarily the same as the number of shares actually issued. For example, a company may have an authorised share capital of £1,000 but have only issued £100 shares.

It would still be entitled to issue the remaining £900 if it wanted to without having to ask the members if they are happy.

With that term no longer in use, since the passing of the 2006 Companies Act, companies are now entitled to issue as many shares as they want.

How do I issue shares – what's involved?

How you actually issue the shares is shown in Appendix 1.11.

Where do I keep share certificates?

Share certificates have a habit of getting lost and so it is not unheard of for the company secretary to be asked to keep them with the statutory books. If individual shareholders wish to keep them, they should be told to keep them securely and in a place of ready access if needed.

Where do I record what shares have been issued?

This is recorded in the register of members.

Do shares need numbering?

No, but you can do so if you wish.

What if a share certificate gets lost?

This can be a real nuisance, which is why we suggest that keeping the certificates under the watchful eye of the company secretary might be a good idea. But, if a share certificate is genuinely lost, before a new certificate can be issued an indemnity must be given. We provide a suggested wording for such an indemnity in Appendix 1.17.

Once this indemnity has been lodged with your company secretary or registered office, the replacement certificate can be issued.

How do I deal with shares held by trustees?

We have just dealt with nominee holdings, and holdings by trusts fall within this category. To repeat what we say there, the shares are issued in the normal manner but a declaration of trust should be completed and the shares entered in the register under the name of the first-named trustee.

What is a declaration of trust?

This is the form that should be prepared when shares are held by nominees. We give a suggested wording in Appendix 1.18.

How do I deal with joint holders of shares?

Where shares are registered in the names of more than one holder – for example, in the case of husband and wife, or when the shares are held by trustees – the maximum number of joint holders is likely to be set at four.

Points that you should be aware of in this regard are:

- the first person named is the one to whom notices of meetings should be sent;

- that person is deemed to be the most senior;

- where more than one joint holder votes at a meeting, only the vote of the senior shareholder is to be counted;

- when shares are transferred, the transfer form must be signed by all joint holders;

- when one of the joint holders dies, the other(s) step into his shoes, which means that the executors of the deceased need not become joint shareholders as well;

- if a joint holder asks for the shares to be split into equal shares, so that each may vote and exercise their rights as individuals, this is allowed. They should all sign the transfer form, the joint holding will therefore be cancelled and the holding split between the joint holders with separate share certificates and declarations of trust being issued.

Making a call on shares

First of all what is a call on shares? The answer is that, when shares are issued, the shareholders are often given the chance of paying for them in instalments or 'calls'.

This can be avoided by issuing a smaller number of shares at the outset and making them fully paid and then issuing more shares later.

But where the shares are paid for in stages, when the next call is due, the board must resolve to authorise the call. See suggested wording for resolution in Appendix 1.12.

Once this has happened a notice must be sent to shareholders and when the cheques are received, the register should be noted accordingly.

If calls remain unpaid, the board may decide to declare the shares, which have not been fully paid for, forfeit.

Can shares be forfeit?

We suppose the first question you will have is, what exactly are forfeit shares and do you need to be bothered with them? First of all forfeit shares are extremely rare nowadays and relate to shares where the shareholder has only partly paid for them and then fails to pay the balance due.

Where this happens, the board has to decide if such shares should be forfeit or cancelled with any or no refund due as a result of the shares not being taken up.

The shareholder must be warned that his shares might be forfeit and we give a suggested wording for this letter in Appendix 1.13.

Once it has been established that the shares will not be paid for in full, the board should resolve to forfeit the shares – again a suggested wording for this forfeiture is given in Appendix 1.14.

The erstwhile shareholder should then be sent a letter informing him of the forfeiture and the relevant notes made in the registers concerned.

How do we increase the share capital in issue (rights issue)?

The only people who may be approached in this connection are existing shareholders; offering additional new shares to an existing shareholder is called a rights issue. In other words the existing shareholders have the right to buy new shares in the company.

We provide a suggested procedure of how to do this in Appendix 1.11b.

If you want to introduce a new member and for him to invest money at a time when the other members are not expected to contribute, this should be done by means of a shareholders' meeting at which they are all asked to approve the membership of this new investor, the number of shares he will buy, the price he will pay and whether or not his shares are to rank the same as the rest of the issued share capital. If the new shares are to be of a different class with different rights, then the shareholders will have to approve the whole new arrangement.

What happens when a shareholder dies?

If a shareholder dies, you should do the following:

1. Ask to see a copy of the probate form or letters of administration. You do not need to see the original probate form, even if your Articles say that you should.

2. Get a letter of request signed by the executor instructing you to register the holding in his name. Once this has arrived, make the entry in the register, even though he should not be called 'executor'. We enclose a sample wording for this letter of request in Appendix 1.16.

3. In due course the shares may be transferred to the new owner (this person will normally be the named beneficiary under the Will). This is done by following the rules for transferring shares (see Appendix 1.35).

What happens when a shareholder marries?

You do not have to register the shares in the married name of the shareholder but if a married woman asks for this to be done, she should be asked to produce her marriage certificate.

Is there a minimum age for a shareholder?

No, there is no minimum age. Infants can hold shares. Such shares should be registered in the name of a parent with the child's initials alongside. When the child reaches 18 the shares can be transferred into the child's own name.

What happens when a shareholder goes bankrupt?

When a shareholder is made bankrupt, a note should be made in the register and the name of the trustee in bankruptcy noted as well.

Do I have to pay Stamp Duty when I issue shares?

Stamp Duty is only paid on the transfer of shares, not when they are issued. Look on the reverse of the transfer form (see Appendix 2.6) where the transfers that are exempt from Stamp Duty are listed. Generally, one-off transactions under £1,000 are exempt.

If you have any doubts about Stamp Duty call the Stamp Duty helpline on 0845 603 0135.

How do I transfer shares from one holder to another?

Please refer to Appendix 1.34.

How can I reduce share capital?

This is permissible but lawyers and accountants will need to be involved, and possibly the court as well. It is also a pretty rare event and only a general outline can be mentioned in this book.

If the court is involved, the procedures that the company secretary has to follow are broadly as follows:

1. Obtain shareholder consent at a general meeting for which special notice has been given. This can be achieved by written resolution.

2. Send a copy of the resolution to Companies House with form SH06.

3. If an inquiry of creditors is required by the court, draw up a list of creditors and prepare to advise them of what is proposed.

4. Once the court has confirmed the reduction, file this confirmation at Companies House.

5. Amend the company's Articles, if this is appropriate.

6. If this reduction causes the name of the company to be changed, ensure that all notices, signs, share certificates and stationery reflect this change.

If the court is not involved, a statement of solvency will need to be prepared but, as we say, you will need independent professional advice.

NB: We do not explain how to carry out the above list of suggested procedures (1. to 6.) because, while we believe them to be helpful, we really do stress our recommendation that it's absolutely vital to employ professional help when reducing share capital.

Can a company buy back the shares in issue from existing shareholders?

This is allowed but it is subject to tax law and so professional advice should be sought. It can be useful when the company has the money to pay for the shares that a shareholder wishes to sell but no other shareholder has the funds available.

In the same way a company can give financial assistance to another party wishing to buy shares in the company but again, professional advice must be sought.

What is a bonus issue and how do I make a bonus issue of shares?

A bonus issue is where the directors decide to convert some of the undistributed reserves into share capital. When this happens the shareholders do not pay for their new shares.

We provide a suggested procedure in Appendix 1.15.

CHAPTER 10
Shareholders' meetings

Before we start this chapter, please remember that shareholders are the same as the members. If you encounter the term 'member', which is used in Table A (the old Articles of Association for most companies incorporated before 1 October 2009), it is synonymous with 'shareholder', the term used in the Model Articles.

How do shareholders take decisions?

There are two ways in which they can take decisions:

1. by holding a meeting at which a resolution is passed; or

2. by passing a written resolution and not holding a meeting.

Types of meeting

There are two types of meeting:

1. Annual General Meetings

2. General meetings

Annual General Meeting

A private company is no longer required to hold an AGM unless the Articles specifically say that one must be held; the new Model Articles have no such requirement.

If the Articles do contain this requirement and the directors or members want to remove it, they should amend the Articles or perhaps adopt the new Model Articles (see Appendix 3.2).

If an AGM is not being held, it will still be necessary to send all members a full set of statutory annual accounts by the last day on which accounts must be delivered to Companies House or the day they are actually delivered to Companies House.

This means that it is now no longer necessary to carry out the following annual duties:

- Laying accounts at a general meeting, whether annual or otherwise.

- Retirement of directors by rotation. Even if this is a requirement of the company's Articles, there is no need for this to happen.

- Annual reappointment of auditors.

As of now auditors are deemed to be reappointed if no resolution to the contrary is passed.

The new Act gives no specific requirements about what should be decided at non-obligatory meetings, so if the shareholders wish to still hold an Annual General Meeting, we give suggested forms of notice and proxy in Appendix 1.21 to 1.25.

General meetings

These may be summoned at any time so long as the required notice is given. This is 14 days for most business matters and 28 days when special notice is required.

We give a suggested notice for a general meeting in Appendix 1.24.

Before any meeting is summoned there should be a board meeting convened to decide on the details of the meeting and to instruct the secretary, or someone else, to send out the notices.

Right to require a shareholders' meeting

Shareholders holding 10 per cent of the voting rights of a company can require the directors to summon a shareholders' meeting and, if there has been no general meeting for 12 months, this is reduced to 5 per cent. The meeting must be held within 28 days of the request being received.

Notice of meeting

The notice period for a shareholders' meeting is now 14 days. If, however, one of six types of resolution is to be considered, special notice of 28 days must be given to the shareholders. These six matters are described below.

However, the 14/28 days' notice are called 'clear days' and this means you must exclude the date of the posting of the notice as well as the date of the meeting itself.

If notice is given electronically (i.e. by email), delivery is deemed to be 48 hours after it is sent. If notice is to be only given electronically, *all* members must have given their consent that this method is acceptable. If some say yes and some say no, then those who say no must be sent notices by post. Those not wishing to be sent such information electronically must still be sent it by post.

A notice may be posted on a website but the shareholders should all have its presence drawn to their attention by email or some other form of communication. This notice must stay on the website until after the meeting has taken place.

What is special notice?

Special notice is 28 days and is now the time or warning that must be given to shareholders if any of the following six matters are to be decided at a shareholders' meeting:

1. to remove a director;

2. to appoint a director other than one who is offering himself for re-election;

3. to appoint as auditor someone other than the current auditor;

4. to fill a casual vacancy in the office of auditor;

5. to reappoint an auditor who was appointed by the directors to fill a casual vacancy; and

6. to remove an auditor before the expiry of his term of office.

The above are usually decided by ordinary resolution, requiring 51 per cent majority.

We give a suggested wording for special notice in Appendix 1.23.

What must the notice contain?

It must contain the following:

- place of meeting;

- date;

- time;

- details of the resolutions to be considered;

- the name of the person sending it out;

- the address from which it has been sent – this is usually the registered office and it makes sense to include all contact details; and

- the date on which it is being dispatched.

We give a sample notice in Appendix 1.21 as well as suggested wording for sending out documents to shareholders.

How to avoid notice

It is possible to circumvent the notice requirements but members holding not less than 90 per cent of the voting rights must agree to short notice of less than 14 days. Be careful because the Articles may provide for a figure in excess of 90 per cent.

This agreement must be evidenced in writing and a suggested specimen wording is given in Appendix 1.25.

How to prepare for an Annual General Meeting

Annual General Meetings are now optional. If you do decide to hold one, these are the things you must remember to do:

1. Send out the notices to members.

2. Send out the accounts to members.

3. Send out the resolutions to members to be discussed.

4. Don't forget to include the directors and the auditor (if there is one) in your list of recipients.

5. Send out proxy forms.

6. Ensure that the venue is ready for the meeting and any refreshments laid on.

7. Take the register of members to the meeting in case there are any queries about someone's holding.

8. Take paper to the meeting so that the minutes can be recorded.

9. Take appropriate slips of paper in case a poll is required. The slips need not be printed.

Remember that the points 1. – 5. must be sent out 14 clear days before the meeting (which really means 16 days before the meeting) and that, if a resolution requires special notice, that must be given to shareholders 28 days (which really means 30 days) before the meeting is due to take place. We give the suggested wording for this letter in Appendix 1.23.

How do I send out the annual accounts to the shareholders?

It makes sense to send out the accounts with notices of any forthcoming meetings and other relevant papers at the same time and we give the suggested wording for this letter in Appendix 1.25.

While on this point, do remember that the accounts you will be sending out will be the final accounts and as such, they might as well be sent to Companies House at the same time. If you do not do this at this stage, there is a danger that the matter may get overlooked with the result that, if the accounts are late, there will be a penalty to pay for late submission and the penalties are now pretty severe.

What to do after the Annual General Meeting

First of all, we give some specimen minutes for an Annual General Meeting in Appendix 1. 26. These must be written up and filed in the appropriate section of the statutory books.

Remember to send details of the relevant resolutions that have been passed to Companies House – see chapter 17.

Adjourning the Annual General Meeting

If the AGM has to be adjourned (perhaps because the accounts are not ready in time), the meeting should still take place but those parts that cannot be dealt with should be carried forward to the adjourned meeting.

Sending resolutions to Companies House

Under the Companies Act 2006 there are now many new forms that must be used for reporting decisions reached and resolutions passed by shareholders. You will find these forms on the Companies House website and we give a list of the more common ones in Appendix 4. We also provide reference to the numbers of the old equivalent forms. You must always now use the new forms.

If there is a resolution you wish to submit for which there is no form available, we provide a template with the wording as required by Companies House, in Appendix 1.27.

What are resolutions?

Resolutions are the decisions that shareholders make and can be divided mainly into ordinary and special.

What are the different types of resolution?

Ordinary

An ordinary resolution requires a simple (51 per cent) majority to be passed. Examples of these include issuing more shares or removing an auditor.

Many ordinary resolutions will need to be submitted to Companies House and we provide a list in chapter 17 of those that are required to be submitted.

Extraordinary

These have been abolished under the Companies Act 2006.

Special

All non-ordinary resolutions are deemed 'special'. These require a 75 per cent majority and in nearly all cases will need to be submitted to Companies House within 15 days of being passed. Examples of these are changing the name of the company, changing the Articles and reducing share capital.

The resolution must state that it is a special resolution.

Elective

These resolutions are no longer appropriate, but we mention them because you may be wondering what's happened to them. They used to be used where a company's Articles required a certain procedure to take place but the procedure concerned was no longer required under the generality of company law. The members could only take advantage of these relaxations if they 'elected' to do so. There is now no longer any need for these resolutions because company law overrides what the Articles may say.

Written

Under the old regime written resolutions had to be signed by 100 per cent of the members. Under the Companies Act 2006, if it's an ordinary resolution, it just needs a simple majority (51 per cent) and if it's a special resolution, it will need to state clearly that it is a special resolution and will need to be passed by a majority of not less than 75 per cent.

To pass a written resolution the following procedure should be followed:

1. Hold a board meeting or pass a written directors' resolution to recommend the matter to shareholders.

2. Circulate the written resolution to all shareholders together with any relevant supporting papers and reports. This can be done by post or electronically, or even using the website.

3. Send a copy to the auditors. This is for information only, because an auditor has no right to vote nor even to require a meeting to be held.

4. The voting can also be done electronically, although it is still more usual for the voting to be done by post in the case of small companies.

5. Once the required majority has been reached the resolution has been passed.

6. Members have one vote per share held.

7. The signed or suitably authenticated copy of the resolution should be filed in the statutory books and, if appropriate, send a copy in the required format to Companies House.

Written resolutions cannot be used for removing a director or auditor. A general meeting must be held for this purpose. This is to enable the person subject to dismissal to be heard by those who have his fate in their hands.

We give the suggested wording for written resolutions in the Appendix 1.27b.

The members can require a written resolution to be subject to a members' meeting. It needs the request of members holding just 10 per cent of voting rights to make such a request effective and binding on the directors.

Single Member Companies can pass all of their resolutions by means of written resolution.

If the company has old Articles (e.g. Table A) where written resolutions require 100 per cent support, it will be necessary to amend the Articles.

What is a quorum for a shareholders' meeting?

A quorum, subject to anything said elsewhere in the company's Articles, will be two. There does not need to be a quorum present throughout the meeting but it does need to be maintained when voting takes place.

If the company has just one member, then a quorum is obviously one.

Who is the chairman of a shareholders' meeting?

You will need to appoint someone to chair a shareholders' meeting and the rules for his behaviour are covered in both Table A and Model Articles.

The directors will normally appoint one of their number to be the chairman and his job is to:

- maintain order;
- see that the items on the agenda are properly dealt with;
- ensure that there is a quorum;
- remove disorderly people;
- decide points of order;
- declare the results of votes;
- order a poll if he is aware that a vote on a show of hands is likely to be reversed in the event of a poll;
- possibly use a casting vote, which, if permitted and used, should normally be cast in favour of the status quo;
- adjourn the meeting if necessary;
- close the meeting.

Does the chairman have a casting vote?

Table A gives the chairman a casting vote but Model Articles do not.

How are votes taken and counted?

Voting is normally done on a show of hands with each member having one vote, no matter how many shares he holds. Proxies are now allowed to vote on a show of hands.

If a poll is required, this means that members vote on slips of paper and under these circumstances the numbers of shares of members is taken into account.

Two or more members or members holding at least 10 per cent of the voting share capital may demand a poll.

A poll may follow after a show of hands and may reverse the earlier decision.

What is a proxy?

A proxy is both a person and a piece of paper.

A proxy (person) is someone appointed by a shareholder to attend the meeting and vote on his behalf.

A proxy (piece of paper) is the form that authorises a proxy to take action and we give a specimen proxy form in Appendix 1.19, and, where these are completed, they must be handed to the company secretary 48 hours before the meeting, excluding weekends and bank holidays. A proxy does not have to be a member.

A proxy may speak at meetings and might even chair a meeting.

If one of the shareholders is itself a company, then that company should appoint someone to represent its interests at the meeting. That company should pass a board resolution (see sample wording in Appendix 1.20) appointing the chosen person or corporate representative to attend the meeting. The representative does not have to complete a proxy form because he is not, strictly speaking, a proxy.

CHAPTER 11

Board meetings

How to hold a board meeting

A company should hold regular board meetings if it is to prove that it is being properly managed. Board meetings should be summoned with proper notice being given and an agenda prepared. You should not hold board meetings on a whim.

The minutes of board meetings should be written up and retained for ten years.

What should a typical board meeting agenda contain?

See suggested wording for a board meeting agenda in Appendix 1.28.

Do all directors have to attend board meetings?

It is definitely advisable for all directors to attend all board meetings, but they can do this by telephone or by video conferencing.

Is there a quorum for board meetings?

The normal quorum for directors' meetings is two, unless the company only has one director.

How is voting counted at board meetings?

Directors will normally have just one vote each and the chairman may have a casting vote. Where a casting vote is used, it should always be used to promote the success of the company, which, in the event of indecision, should be used to preserve the status quo.

Written resolutions may be used by directors.

The importance of board meetings

If a company becomes insolvent it will be important to show that regular board meetings were held, that there was a regular programme for holding them with well-prepared agendas and up-to-date information and regular reviews of the company's performance.

CHAPTER 12

Accounts

The form and content of a company's statutory accounts is regulated by various accounting standards, as well as the Companies Act 2006. It is the directors' responsibility to ensure that accounts are prepared in accordance with the Companies Act, and if the company requires an audit, the company's auditors must also confirm this.

Every company is required by the Companies Act 2006 to keep adequate accounting records, sufficient to show and explain the company's transactions and to:

- disclose with reasonable accuracy at any time the financial position of the company at that time; and

- enable the directors to ensure that any accounts required to be prepared comply with the requirements of the Companies Act 2006.

The accounting records must, in particular, contain:

- up-to-date entries of all sums of money received and expended by the company; and

- a record of the assets and liabilities of the company.

This point is now extremely important, because HM Revenue & Customs, to whom accounts must be sent when the Corporation Tax liability is being assessed, is now issuing fines of up to £3,000 for poor record-keeping.

Accounting reference date

When the company is incorporated, it is automatically given an accounting reference date of the end of the month it was incorporated, for example, a company incorporated on 12 June, unless this is changed, will have a year end date of 30 June.

The maximum period for submitting the company's first set of accounts is 22 months from the date of incorporation and the maximum period for which a set of accounts may be prepared is 18 months, unless the company is in administration.

How can I change the accounting reference date?

To change the accounting reference date you must complete form AA01. This can only be done if the current set of accounts is not already late. This can either be submitted online or downloaded from the Companies House website and sent by post.

There are no rules for reducing the length of time for a set of accounts, but you are only allowed to extend the period once every five years, unless you have permission from the government, are in administration or are bringing the year end into line with a group within the EU.

Filing deadlines and fines

The deadline for submitting a set of accounts to Companies House depends on the company's year end and type of company.

For a private limited company, if the current accounting period began on or after 6 April 2009, then the company must submit its accounts within nine months after the start of its accounting period. If the company's accounting period spans 6 April 2009, then the company will have ten months after the accounting period end to submit the accounts. The deadline for public companies to submit accounts is six months from 6 April 2009, seven months before 6 April 2009.

It is worth noting that if the accounting period is shortened, then the deadline for submitting the accounts is shortened by the same timescale. This is also the same if the reference date is extended; the deadline is extended by the same timescale.

The current late filing penalties are:

Period late	Private company	Public company
Not more than one month	£150	£750
More than one month but less than three months	£375	£1,500
More than three months but less than six months	£750	£3,000
More than six months	£1,500	£7,500

You may have glossed over the above chart, but do look again. Do you realise that if you are over one month late (yes, just one month late) the automatic penalty will be £375? It is a huge sea-change in the penalties that directors now have to get used to.

And, if that were not bad enough, there is an extra new sting in the tail from the Companies Act 2006 in the form of double fines. If the accounts are submitted late one period and then submitted late the next period, the fine for the second period will be doubled.

Do I need an auditor?

The current small company audit exemption limits are:

* Annual turnover less than £6.5 million.

* Balance sheet total no more than £3.26 million.

If a company breaks just one of the above limits, then it must have an audit. However, even if it passes both of the above tests, if a company is part of a group, is a Public Limited company or is subject to a statute-based regime (e.g. the Financial Services Authority) then it may not be able to claim exemption from having an audit.

A company can also not claim exemption if 10 per cent of the shareholders have vetoed the exemption; if 10 per cent ask for an audit, one must be undertaken.

If a company is able to take advantage of an audit exemption, the director must state this in the accounts.

What are small and medium-sized companies?

Please be aware that the point of whether a company is 'small' or 'medium-sized' for this purpose is not to do with whether it needs an audit or not, but whether it is entitled to submit accounts to Companies House which contain less information.

These are the thresholds:

	Small	Medium-sized
Annual turnover	£6.5 million	£25.9 million
Balance sheet total	£3.26 million	£12.9 million
Average number of employees	50	250

If a company breaks two or more of the above thresholds, then it will not qualify as a small or medium-sized company.

Again, there are companies which cannot claim this exemption, such as public companies, those that are part of an ineligible group and those which are subject to a statute-based regime.

Who signs the accounts?

The persons who should sign the relevant reports are:

- Directors' report: a director or secretary of the company.

- Balance Sheet: a director of the company.

- Auditor's report: audit partner.

What accounts are filed at Companies House?

There are generally two different types of statutory accounts that can be submitted to Companies House:

Full accounts: These include a large amount of information on the company for the period and are generally only submitted to Companies House if an audit is required or the company does not qualify as small or medium-sized.

Abbreviated accounts: These accounts have considerably less information than full sets, and offer the owners more anonymity and are only available to small and medium-sized companies that qualify for exemption. There are different requirements of abbreviated sets of accounts for small and medium-sized companies.

This book will not go into detail as to what should be included in a set of accounts due to the complexity of the various statutes. If you require assistance with this, we would suggest contacting an accountant.

Dormant company accounts

If a company was created to 'buy' a name and so stop others using that name, or was incorporated, but is not going to be used, then it may be able to submit dormant company accounts.

A company can be classed as dormant if the following transactions are the only transactions which have taken place in the period:

- Payment of shares taken by the subscribers.

- Payment of a civil penalty for late filing of accounts.

- Fees for the Annual Return, change of name and the re-registration of a company.

If any other transactions have taken place, then a full set of accounts must be prepared.

For companies that have not traded since incorporation they may be able to submit accounts on form AA02. If a company has traded and is now classed as dormant, then the company will not be able to use this form and will have to submit dormant accounts that can be best described as an abbreviated set of accounts for the period.

CHAPTER 13

Auditors

Do I need an auditor?

Few private companies need an audit nowadays and for an explanation of which companies are exempt, please turn to chapter 12.

How do I appoint an auditor?

Auditors can be appointed by the board of directors for a term of office, usually until the completion of the audit of the upcoming or current set of accounts.

An auditor is entitled to receive notice of all shareholders' meetings and indeed to attend them. He may even speak at general meetings on issues that concerns him.

He can even insist on calling a general meeting when he resigns, and if there are circumstances that should be brought to the attention of the members or creditors.

How do I dismiss an auditor?

An auditor can be removed before the expiry of his term of office by ordinary resolution of which special notice must have been given. Notice of such a resolution being passed must be submitted to Companies House on form AA03.

Special notice must be given to the auditor who is being removed and he must give written representation to the company explaining any circumstances which he feels should be brought to the members' attention. If there are no circumstances this must also be stated and this statement should be sent to the company within 14 days of the auditor receiving notice that it is intended to remove him.

The auditor must send a copy of this statement to the Registrar of Companies within 28 days of depositing it with the company.

A resolution appointing someone other than the existing auditor also requires special notice.

How can an auditor resign?

An auditor may resign at any time but, if he does, he must send his resignation in writing to the registered office giving details of any circumstances in connection with his resignation. If there are no reasons, he should say so.

The company should send a copy of this notice to Companies House within 14 days of receiving it.

CHAPTER 14

Business stationery

What business stationery must show

All business stationery, order forms, emails, websites, etc., must include the following information:

- The company name, including the word 'limited'.

- The place of its registration (England and Wales, Scotland or Northern Ireland).

- Its registered number.

- The address of its registered office.

In addition it's also sensible to include:

- Its address, if it's not the same as the registered office.

- Contact details such as website, phone and fax numbers, etc.

- VAT number, if appropriate.

If the names of directors are included, then all of the names must be printed. It's unwise to print the names of all directors because if one ceases to act, it will necessitate the reprinting of all business stationery.

An investment company must state that it is one on its stationery.

Where a company is entitled to dispense with using the word 'limited' it must state on its business stationery somewhere that it is thus entitled. If a charity that is also a limited company does not have the word 'charity' in its name, it should state the fact that it is a charity on its business stationery.

CHAPTER 15

Mortgages and charges

If the company has any borrowing powers, these will have been laid down in the company Articles.

While the following will not apply to overdrafts, loans and mortgages taken out must be reported to Companies House on form MG01 within 21 days and the details of any property subject to a charge must be submitted on form MG08.

You may find that your lender insists on submitting the forms to Companies House itself because, if the charge, etc. is not registered at Companies House, it will be invalid and the charge will not be enforceable against the company.

When a mortgage or charge has been entered into, the details must be recorded in a register of charges – see sample layout in Appendix 1.30g.

When the charge is repaid or discharged, there are a number of different Companies Act forms that might be required and their use is beyond the scope of this book. Professional advice should be sought.

CHAPTER 16
Dividends

What is a dividend?

A dividend is a proportion of the distributable profits which the company pays to its shareholders. A company may not distribute more than its distributable profits.

The directors declare any interim dividend paid during the year but, historically, the shareholders have declared, or confirmed, the amount of the final dividend after the end of the year once the figure of distributable profits is known. Under Model Articles it is now the directors that declare all dividends.

The shareholders cannot insist on being paid a dividend.

The usual precaution when declaring a dividend is not to distribute more than two-thirds of the profits after tax has been deducted.

We show the procedure for declaring a dividend, plus the suggested layout for a dividend voucher and bank mandate for paying dividends, in Appendix 1.5 to 1.7.

How to waive a dividend

As already intimated, a shareholder is entitled to waive his right to receive a dividend. Where this happens he should lodge a document as shown in Appendix 1.6. Such action can lead to adverse tax consequences and so professional advice should be sought.

What are 'scrip dividends'?

Scrip dividends are where, instead of cash being paid to shareholders, they are given more shares in proportion to the number already held. The money still comes from distributable reserves and professional advice should be sought. They are sometimes called 'bonus issues'. See also chapter 9.

CHAPTER 17

Other matters

Companies House

What is it?

Companies House was created in 1844, and its main functions today are:

- incorporating and dissolving limited companies;

- examining and storage of company information delivered under the Companies Act and related legislation;

- making the above information available to the public.

There are four Companies House offices and their addresses are:

For England and Wales:

Registrar of Companies
Companies House
Crown Way
Cardiff CF14 3UZ

For Scotland:

Registrar of Companies
Companies House, Fourth Floor
Edinburgh Quay 2
139 Fountainbridge
Edinburgh EH3 9FF

For Northern Ireland:

The Registrar of Companies
Companies House
Second Floor
The Linenhall
32–38 Linenhall Street
Belfast BT2 8BG

London Information Centre:

Companies House Executive Agency
21 Bloomsbury Street
London WC1B 3XD

As mentioned above, Companies House stores all the information it is sent and makes it available for the public to view. In describing how this works it would be as well to review the online services that Companies House now offers:

The web filing service

Companies House has a very good web filing service where many forms such as Annual Return forms for issuing of shares and changing the company's officers can be submitted. You have to register with Companies House for online filing and once the company has been registered for online filing, an online authentication code is sent to the company's registered office in approximately five days. This will be required for the submission of forms online and it will involve the use of a code of six letters and numbers.

Forms submitted online usually find their way onto the public register within 25 minutes. Such forms are much more secure than when sent by post.

Protected Online Filing (PROOF)

If you are registered for PROOF you will have much better protection against identity fraud. If your company is registered for PROOF (you do this online), Companies House will no longer accept paper documents for your company.

Webcheck

This provides visitors to the Companies House website with information on all registered companies. Some of the information is free.

You can search for any registered limited company in the UK. Once on the company's main screen, you will have the option to purchase various items. To view a list of all the forms that have been submitted to Companies House for that company, click on 'order information on this company'. To purchase any items you need to register with Companies House. There is no charge for registering.

Monitor

This service allows you to monitor any company on the register. The moment there's a development (such as a new director being appointed or the latest set of accounts being filed) you will be sent an email. This service used to cost 50p per company per year, but has been free since 6 April 2011.

Resolutions that need to be submitted to Companies House

In principle, all resolutions that are not one of the following four need to be submitted to Companies House within 15 days of being passed:

1. declaring a dividend (now decided by directors in any event);

2. receiving accounts;

3. election of directors (there is now a number of special forms for submitting this information to Companies House in any event);

4. appointing auditors.

Just to make it absolutely clear, the above four resolutions do NOT have to be submitted, although, in the case of a change in directors or a director's details, these must be submitted to Companies House on a form such as AP01 or CH01.

This means that the following 16 resolutions definitely need to be submitted to Companies House:

1. Any special resolution.

2. Change of name.

3. Change of Articles.

4. Remove an auditor.

5. Remove a director.

6. Re-registration from private to public and from limited to unlimited.

7. Vary the rights of a class of shareholders.

8. Reduce capital.

9. Purchase own shares.

10. Decision to wind up.

11. Disposal of the company's books.

12. Authority to purchase own shares out of capital.

13. Allotment of securities.

14. Disapplication of pre-emption rights.

15. Varying the name of shares.

16. Capitalisation or a bonus issue of shares.

Limited Liability Partnerships

Limited Liability Partnerships (LLPs) are still relatively rare and we will only deal with them briefly in this book. Here are their salient points:

- They are very similar to limited companies but they have the flexibility of a partnership.

- They can be formed by two or more people carrying on a lawful business. Such people are called members, and members can also be firms as well as people.

- Two of the members will be called 'designated members' whose details, and any changes in those details, must be submitted to Companies House.

- Designated members have the same rights and duties as non-designated members but they have additional responsibilities such as appointing an auditor, signing the accounts, delivering accounts and the Annual Return, and notifying Companies House of any changes.

- They are not available for charities.

- An existing company may not be converted into an LLP.

- They are entitled to limited liability, which means the liability of the members is limited.

- They are taxed as a partnership.

- They must have a registered office.

- If the number of members falls below two and remains as such for more than six months, they will lose the benefits of limited liability.

- The name of the business must end with the words 'limited liability partnership'.

- The name must be displayed in the same manner as a limited company's name.

- LLPs must display the same details on their stationery, websites, emails, etc. as those for limited companies.

- LLPs must make their accounts and registers available for inspection.

- LLPs are liable to similar penalties for late submission of accounts, etc.

- The accounts for LLPs must be prepared according to statutory rules.

Second filing of a document previously delivered

In the past, if a Companies Act 1985 form was sent into Companies House with, for example, incorrect spelling of a surname or incorrect title, to correct this a new form would have had to be sent in, with 'AMENDED' written across the top of it. However, for the Companies Act 2006, the system has changed for certain forms (Appointing a director/secretary [AP01-04], Change of director/secretary's [CH01-04], Termination of director/secretary [TM01-02], Allotment of shares [SH01] and the Annual Return [AR01]). You will still need to send in an amended form, but you must also submit form RP04- Second filing of a document previously delivered.

Community Interest Companies (CICs)

Although not covered in detail in this book, we feel the need to mention that when submitting a set of CIC accounts to Companies House, they must be accompanied by a cheque for £15 made payable to Companies House and form CIC34. Copies of form CIC34 are available from www.cicregulator.gov.uk. After corresponding with the CIC regulator, we were informed that in most cases the 'Simplified Community Interest Company Report' would be sufficient for small companies.

APPENDIX 1

Suggested procedures and templates

1.1 Pre-incorporation checklist

1.2 Investors' Aspiration Form

1.3 The likely headings in a shareholders' agreement

1.4 Notices – how to display
    a. Particulars of Ownership – how to display
    b. Situation of registered office

1.5 Dividends
    a. How to pay a dividend
    b. Dividend tax voucher

1.6 Waiver and release of dividend

1.7 Dividend mandate

1.8 Application form for shares

1.9 Letter of allotment

1.10 Letter of regret

1.11 Share issue
    a. How to issue the first shares
    b. How to issue additional shares (rights issue)
    c. Board resolution to allot shares

1.12 Board resolution making a call on shares

1.13 Letter warning of possible forfeiture

1.14 Board resolution forfeiting shares

1.15 Bonus issue
    a. How to make a bonus issue of shares
    b. Board resolution

1.1 | Pre-incorporation checklist

Please complete in capital letters

Preferred name_____

What will the company be doing? _____

Issued share capital   £ _____

This is the sum that will have to be paid for the shares.

Please note below how many shares are to be issued to each shareholder.

Accounting year end   _____

This will normally be the anniversary of the end of the month in which the company is first registered. Leave this line blank if you are not bothered by which year end the company has.

'Additional information', see page 75

Names of shareholders

Name	_____	No	Detail
Address	_____		
	_____		
Phone	_____		
No of shares to be issued to this shareholder	_____		

Name	_____	No	Detail
Address	_____		
	_____		
Phone	_____		
No of shares to be issued to this shareholder	_____		

Name	_____	No	Detail
Address	_____		
	_____		
Phone	_____		
No of shares to be issued to this shareholder	_____		

1.1 | Pre-incorporation checklist (cont)

Name	_____	No	Detail
Address	_____		
	_____		
Phone	_____		

No of shares to be
issued to this shareholder _____

Names of directors and please indicate who is to be the chairman

Name _____

Nationality _____ Date of birth _____

Address _____

_____

Phone _____

Occupation _____

		No	Detail

Name _____

Nationality _____ Date of birth _____

Address _____

_____

Phone _____

Occupation _____

		No	Detail

Name of the company secretary (if applicable)

Name _____

Nationality _____ Date of birth _____

Address _____

_____

Phone _____

Occupation _____

		No	Detail

Address of the registered office. *This can't be a PO Box number.*

Address _____

_____

_____

1.1 | Pre-incorporation checklist (cont)

Additional information needed for all directors, all shareholders and the company secretary

Please select three of the following and enter both number and detail against the appropriate name above.

1. First three letters of town of birth
2. First three letters of mother's maiden name
3. First three letters of father's first forename
4. Last three digits of home telephone number
5. Last three digits of National Insurance number
6. Last three digits of passport number
7. First three letters of eye colour

1.2 | Investors' Aspiration Form

How well are the intended participators going to work together?

We suggest that everyone takes a copy of this list and writes his answers down for an independent and knowledgeable person to review and report on how well it appears everyone will work together in the new business:

Name of person completing this form	
Questions	**Answers**
What do I hope this business will achieve?	
Why do I think this business will be successful?	
What will I bring to the business in terms of opening capital for shares and any other assets?	
How much time will I devote to the business?	
What would I like to do in the business?	
What title would I like to have?	
What do I not want to do in the business?	
Who do I think the boss of the business should be?	
Will I be prepared to bring more money to the business should it be necessary to do so?	
When would I like to retire from the business?	
What do I hope to earn from the business each year?	
What dividends I would hope to be paid?	
What benefits would I like the business to provide.? E.g. a car, mobile phone.	
What would I like to happen to my shares in the event of my early death?	
Who should sign cheques, etc.?	
Over what level of payment should a cheque have more than one signature?	
Where should the business bank?	
Should accounts be prepared more frequently than annually?	
Which firm of accountants should be appointed?	
Should there be a shareholders' agreement?	

1.2 | Investors' Aspiration Form (cont)

Signed_____Date_____

Once the copies of these forms are complete, hand them to your chosen reviewer for him to look at, compare and then give his candid opinion of whether the people involved are likely to work well together, as well as to highlight where any potential difficulties appear to lie. The sort of person we have in mind to conduct this review might be a partner in the company's chosen firm of chartered accountants.

1.3 | The likely headings in a shareholders' agreement

Date_____ 20_____

Shareholder 1   _____

and

Shareholder 2   _____

            and others if appropriate

SHAREHOLDERS' AGREEMENT

Relating to

ABC Limited

Parties

1.   Shareholder 1 of (address) and

2.   Shareholder 2 of (address)

3.   Etc. i.e. further shareholders, if appropriate

The agreement will then contain sections such as the following:

1.   Definitions
   1.   Articles   The Articles of Association of the company
   2.   Shares   The ordinary shares of the company
   3.   Board   The board of directors of the company

2.   The business of the company
   The shareholders agree that the business of the company shall be XYZ. The shareholders agree to co-operate with each other in the running and operation of the company to achieve the company's objects and to act reasonably and in good faith.

3.   Management practice
   Who will be responsible for which aspects of the company (production, marketing, administration, finance, etc.)

4.   Spending restrictions and cheque signatures

5.   Managing the business (what must not be done unless agreed by a majority of shareholders)

1.3 | The likely headings in a shareholders' agreement (cont)

6. **Accounts – responsibility for preparing**

7. **Other contracts – if appropriate – e.g. directors' service contracts**

8. **Continuance – length of agreement**

9. **Partnership – that this agreement is not a partnership deed**

10. **Assignment of responsibilities – whether this is allowed**

11. **Arbitration – resolving disputes**

12. **Confidentiality**

13. **Waiver or amendment of terms within this agreement**

14. **Managing the business (what must not be done unless agreed by majority of shareholders)**

In witness whereof the parties to this agreement have duly executed this agreement on the day and year written above.

Signed by Shareholder 1 _____

Witnessed by _____

Address _____

_____

Signed by Shareholder 2 _____

Witnessed by _____

Address _____

_____

1.4a | Notices | Particulars of Ownership – how to display

Notice of Particulars of Ownership

As required by section 1202 of the Companies Act 2006

_____

[*Insert name of business*]

Proprietors

_____

[*Insert name of proprietors*]

Address within Great Britain at which documents may be

effectively served on the proprietor in relation to the business

_____

_____

_____

[*Insert full address*]

1.4b | Notices | Situation of registered office

Welcome to

_____Ltd

You are now at 123 High Street
Anytown
Anyshire
AN12 3YZ

This is the address of our registered office.

_____

Secretary

1.5a | How to pay a dividend

The directors pass a board minute that might be worded:

'That an interim dividend of x pence per share for the year ended [*date*] be declared payable on
____/____/20____ to shareholders registered as such on the register at close of business on
____/____/20____.'

Once this has been done:

- A list of the dividends payable must be drawn up.

- You should check to see if there have been any requests for dividends to be paid to someone other than a shareholder.

- You should also check to see if anyone has chosen to waive (i.e. not receive) his dividend.

- It may be a good idea to open a new bank account for dividend payments.

- Perhaps some dividends can be paid by bank transfer or other automated means.

- Prepare the cheques that are needed.

- Prepare the dividend vouchers (see sample 5b).

- Send out dividend vouchers and cheques.

It is no longer normal practice to close the shareholders' register while this procedure is followed.

1.5b | Dividend tax voucher

Statement to accompany dividend cheque showing tax credit

Company name _____Limited

Company number _____

Registered office address _____

_____

Date _____

Dear Sir or Madam

Holder of _____ (ordinary) shares

An interim/final dividend* at the rate of [x] pence per share on the (ordinary) shares of the company has been duly declared for the year ended _____[date].

We enclose a cheque for £_____

Or

We have today paid to your bank to the credit of your account the sum of £_____ being the amount of the dividend due in respect of your above shareholding.

The rate of dividend payable is £___:___p per (ordinary) shares.

There is a tax credit associated with this dividend equal to £_____.

This dividend together with the associated tax credit is equivalent to a gross amount of £_____.

This statement should be retained and will be accepted by HM Revenue & Customs as evidence of a tax credit.

Signed

_____

Secretary

*An interim dividend is one paid during a financial year. A final dividend is one paid after the end of a financial year.

1.6 | Waiver and release of dividend

I, _____

of _____ , the registered holder

of [*number*] _____ ordinary shares of £ _____ each, in the capital of

_____ Limited, (the Company).

(i)   waive all right to participate by reason of my ordinary shares as noted above in all dividends whether interim, final or otherwise declared by the Company or its directors; and

(ii) release into the Company such sums as would have been payable from time to time by way of dividend on my ordinary shares as noted above.

Please apply this waiver and release to all dividends attributable to me and declared until I revoke this waiver by notice in writing to the Company at its registered office provided that such dividends shall be declared and become payable within 12 months of the date of this notice.

Date _____

Signed _____

_____   _____
Shareholder's signature   Witness' signature

_____   _____
Shareholder's name in full   Witness' name in full

Address _____

_____

_____

_____

Occupation

1.7 | Dividend mandate

Request for payment of interest or dividends

Name of company in which shares are held _____Limited.

Full name and address of the first-named holder. *Where shares are in the name of a deceased holder, instructions signed by the executor(s) or administrator(s) should indicate the name of the deceased.*

First-named holder _____

Address_____

Account designation (if any) _____

Postcode _____

Full name(s) of other holders (including deceased if applicable)

Second-named holder _____   Third-named holder _____

Fourth-named holder_____   Name of deceased _____
                                             (if applicable)

Signatures of shareholder(s)

First-named holder_____   Second-named holder _____

Third-named holder _____   Fourth-named holder _____

In the case of corporate shareholders the signatory should indicate the capacity in which they are signing (e.g. director).

Name and address of bank, building society or person: _____

Please pay future interest or dividends for the above company directly to the following or to any other bank/building society which that organisation may instruct.

*Name of institution/person you wish to pay your dividends to*_____

Account name _____   Address _____

Branch sort code _____   Postcode _____

Account number_____   Building society
                                          reference/roll number _____
                                          (if applicable)

1.8 | Application form for shares

To the directors of _____Limited.

I/we enclose a cheque for the sum of £ _____, being payment of _____ per share on application for [*number*] _____ preference/ordinary shares of £_____ each in the capital of your company.

Please allot me/us with the appropriate number of shares.

I/we undertake and agree to accept either the above number of shares or any lesser number that may be allotted to me/us and I/we would be grateful if you would enter my/our name(s) on the register of members of the company as the holder(s) of the said shares.

Please send a letter of allotment in respect of these shares and, if appropriate, a cheque for any refund due to the first address written below.

I understand that any shares for which I apply but for which I have not paid in full may be forfeit.

Full name(s) _____

Address in full _____

Usual signature _____

Other joint holder(s)

Full name(s) _____

Address in full _____

Usual signature _____

Please note that applications must be made in the names of individuals or corporations, and not in the name of partnerships.

This form, when completed, must be sent with a remittance for the amount payable on application to _____ [*company secretary/other*] at _____ [*registered office address/or registrars' address*] not later than _____20___.

Cheques should be made payable to '_____ Limited' and crossed 'A/c payee only'.

Please note that no receipt will be issued for the payment, but an acknowledgement will be forwarded in due course either by letter of allotment in whole or in part, or by the issue of the share certificate, or by return of some or all of the application money.

1.9 | Letter of allotment

No _____ : in case of enquiry please quote this number.

This document is of value, it should be kept carefully. It will be exchanged for a share certificate in due course.

_____**Limited**

Registered in England. Company registration

_____

Address of registered office

_____

To [*name of person applying for shares*] _____

of [*address*] _____

In response to your application for shares in this company, the directors have allotted to you _____ [*number*] shares.

The amount required to pay up the said shares in full is £ _____. You have paid on application £ _____, leaving a balance due to you for which a cheque is enclosed for £ _____.

This letter of allotment is not renounceable, which means that you cannot transfer this allotment to another person. If you wish to transfer the shares, once the certificate has been issued to you, this should be done by means of a duly stamped transfer form. If you wish to do this, please ask us for a transfer form. Please be aware that, this being a private company, the directors have to approve the person to whom you propose to transfer any shares.

Pending the issue of share certificates, transfers will be certified at the registered office of the company against surrender of this letter of allotment duly receipted.

Share certificates will be ready for issue in exchange for letters of allotment duly receipted on or after _____[*date*] at the registered office of the company.

By order of the board

_____

Secretary

1.10 | Letter of regret

From _____ Limited

To _____

of _____[address]

Dear Sir or Madam

Thank you for applying for shares in the above company, but I regret to inform you that in view of the oversubscription you have not been successful and we are unable to offer you any shares.

I enclose a cheque for £_____ representing the sum that you paid with your application form.

Yours faithfully

_____

Secretary

1.11a | How to issue the first shares

We suggest that you:

i. Gather up all the applications for shares, number them and file them (see suggested application form 8 above).

ii. List them in the applications and allotments register.

iii. Hold a board meeting to approve of the proposed share allotment (see 1.11c below).

iv. Prepare letters of allotment (see suggested procedure in form 1.9 above) and check them against the applications in the book.

v. Dispatch the letters to those who have been allotted shares.

vi. Send letters of regret to those who have not been fortunate to be allocated shares (see 1.10 above).

vii. Prepare return of allotments form SH01 and send to Companies House.

viii. Make the entries in the register of shareholders. Prepare an index if there are more than 50 members.

ix. Prepare share certificates and, after obtaining the consent of the board, date them. Seal them as well if you have a company seal.

x. Either dispatch the share certificates to the new members or, if they agree that you, the company secretary, should hold them for safe keeping and convenience, file them safely.

1.11b | How to issue additional shares in an existing company (rights issue)

To increase share capital by asking existing shareholders to invest more money should be done as follows:

i. Hold a board meeting to agree to this proposal.

ii. Write to all the members with an application form for this proposed new allotment (you could use form 1.8). Existing shareholders will be offered a number of new shares in proportion to the number of their existing holding.

iii. When the application forms have been completed and returned, list them in the allotments book.

iv. Hold a board meeting to approve the allotments.

v. Prepare the letters of allotment and send them to the shareholders who have indicated that they wish to invest further sums in the company.

vi. Send letters of regret to those who will not be allocated new shares.

vii. Prepare form SH01 and send to Companies House within one month of the allotment being completed.

viii. Amend the register of shareholders in accordance with the new issue.

ix. Prepare share certificates and send them out.

x. If certain members decline to buy their full quota of the new issue, the unallocated shares can be offered to the other shareholders and this is normally done on a first-come first-served basis.

1.11c | Board resolution to allot shares

_____Ltd

The following applications for allotments of shares havebeen received, together with the payments noted:

[_List here or on a separate sheet_]

It was resolved THAT:

a)   _____ [_number_] shares of £_____ each and fully paid be allotted to the applicants above;

b)   the relevant share certificates be issued; and

c)   form SH01 be filed at Companies House.

Signed_____

Director/secretary

Date_____

1.12 | Board resolution making a call on shares

_____Ltd

It was resolved:

THAT a call of _____ [amount] pence per share be made on _____
[number] shares payable on_____ [date] to the company at its account
with_____Bank PLC at   _____ [address].

Signed_____

Director/secretary

Date_____

1.13 | Letter warning of possible forfeiture

On company letterhead

To: Name   _____

       Date   _____

       Address   _____

Dear Sir or Madam

This is to remind you that the call on shares held by you in this company made on _____[*date*] and amounting to £_____ has not yet been received.

The board now requires you to pay this sum in accordance with the Articles of Association together with interest at the rate of _____ per cent per annum on or before _____[*date*].

I therefore give you notice that, if you do not make payment of £_____ by the due date, your shares on which the call is made will be forfeited in accordance with the Articles of Association, together with all dividends declared in respect of such shares. (In addition, you will remain liable to pay any sums due in respect of such shares notwithstanding the forfeiture.)

By order of the board

_____

Secretary

1.14 | Board resolution forfeiting shares

_____Ltd

It was resolved that:

_____ [name], the holder of _____ shares in the above company, on which _____ [partly paid amount] per share has been paid, having failed to pay the call made by the board on_____ [date], and due on _____ [date] and having failed to comply with the notice served upon them on [date], the shares mentioned above to be declared forfeited.

Note: If there are a large number of holders who have not paid the call, the above resolution could be adapted to refer to a schedule of their names, number of shares and other details which could be produced to the meeting.

Signed_____

Director/secretary

Date_____

1.15 | Bonus issue

a.   How to make a bonus issue of shares

If you want to make a bonus issue, while professional advice should be sought, these are the procedures to follow:

a.   Start off by passing a board resolution – see suggested sample below.

b.   Then get the members' agreement at a general meeting – we also provide a suggested wording for that below.

c.   Once passed issue the new shares to the members as appropriate.

d.   File form SH01 with a copy of the approved resolution at Companies House.

e.   Allot the new shares and amend the register accordingly.

b.   Board resolution

That the sum of £_____ in the company's distributable reserves be distributed to existing members in the form of _____additional free shares for _____already held.

c.   Members' resolution to approve a bonus issue

(to be passed by members/shareholders)

_____Ltd

We resolve that

a.   It is beneficial to capitalise the sum of £_____ standing in the profit and loss account and accordingly that such sum be freed for distribution among the holders of ordinary shares of the company on condition that the same be not paid in cash but be used in paying up in full _____ ordinary shares of £ _____ each of the company, to be allotted and distributed and credited as fully paid up to and among such holders in the proportion of _____ new ordinary shares for every ordinary share held by them respectively.

b.   Should any holder of ordinary shares be entitled to a fraction of a new ordinary share the same shall be ignored.

c.   The shares issued following this resolution shall carry the same rights as, and rank equally in every respect with, all other ordinary shares of the company including the right to participate in full in all dividends declared on the ordinary share capital of the company.

1.16 | Death of a shareholder

Suggested letter of request*

Request by a deceased holder's executors or administrators to be registered as members of the company

To the directors of_____ Limited

Re _____Dec'd, former shareholder in your company

Re his holding of _____ shares in the above-named company.

I/we, the undersigned, being the personal representative(s) of the above-named deceased, request you to register me/us in the books of the company as the holder(s) of the above-mentioned shares presently registered in the name of the said deceased.

Dated this _____ day of _____20_____

Signatures(s) of personal representative(s)

_____

_____

Please complete this form in typescript or block capitals entering full name(s) and full postal address(es) (including postcode(s)) of the personal representative(s) in the order in which he/they is/are to be registered.

Please state title, if any, or whether Mr/Mrs/Miss/Ms.

If an account already exists in the above name(s) the above-mentioned holding will be added to that account, unless instructions are received to the contrary.

The share certificate(s) in the name of the deceased if not already with the company or its registrar must accompany this form.

*A separate letter of request should be used for each class of security.

1.17 | Indemnity for lost share certificate(s)

Form to be used if the original certificate is not available for surrender to the company

To the directors of_____ Limited (the 'Company')

The original certificate(s) of title relating to the securities of the Company noted below has/ve been destroyed or lost.

As far as I/we are aware, neither the securities nor the certificate(s) of title to them have been transferred, charged, lent or deposited or dealt with in any manner which affects the absolute title to them and I/we confirm that the person(s) named in the said certificate(s) is/are the person(s) entitled to be on the register in respect of such securities.

I/we request that you issue a duplicate certificate(s) of title for such securities and, in consideration of your doing so, we undertake (jointly and severally) to indemnify you and the Company against all claims and demands (and any related expenses) which may be made against you or the Company as a result of your compliance with this request and of the Company permitting at any time afterwards a transfer of the said securities, or any of them, without the production of the said original certificate(s).

I/we undertake to forward to the Company the said original certificate(s) for cancellation should the same ever be recovered.

Particulars of certificate(s) lost or destroyed

Particulars of certificate   _____

Amount and class of securities   _____

In favour of (name of holder)   _____

Dated this _____ day of _____ 20 ____

Signature(s) _____

*We   _____

hereby join in the above indemnity and undertaking.

*Bank, insurance company, etc.

1.18 | Declaration of trust

This form may be used when shares are in the name of someone other than their owner. Stamp Duty is payable, currently at the rate of £5.

DECLARATION OF TRUST

THIS DECLARATION OF TRUST IS MADE the _____ day of _____ 20 _____

BETWEEN _____

of [*address*] _____('the Trustee/Nominee')

and _____

of [*address*]_____('the Owner').

WHEREAS:

1. The owner is the beneficial owner of _____ ordinary shares of [£ *amount*]in the share capital of _____ Limited (company no _____) whose registered office is situated at _____ .

2. The Owner caused this share to be issued in the name of the Trustee/Nominee.

3. The Trustee/Nominee acknowledges that the share was issued to them as nominee of the owner and that they hold the share(s) upon trust for the owner absolutely.

4. The power to appoint new Trustees/Nominees is vested in the owner.

IN WITNESS whereof the parties have today set their hands and seals

SIGNED as a deed and DELIVERED by the said _____

in the presence of   _____

Witness name   _____

Address   _____

Occupation   _____

1.19 | Proxy form

_____Limited

Proxy form for use by ordinary shareholders of the above company

at the Annual General Meeting (AGM)

to be held on _____ [_date_]

Please read the notice of meeting carefully before completing this form.

As a member of _____ Limited you have the right to attend, speak at and vote at the AGM. If you cannot or do not wish to attend the AGM but still want to vote, you can appoint someone to attend and vote on your behalf. That person is known as a 'proxy'. You can use the proxy form to appoint the chairman of the meeting or someone else as your proxy. Your proxy does not have to be a member of the company.

I/we _____ [_insert full name in block capitals_],

being a member(s) of _____Limited, appoint the chairman of the meeting or_____ [_see note 1 overleaf_] as my/our proxy to attend and vote for me/us and on my/our behalf as indicated below at the AGM and at any adjournment (see notes 2 and 3 overleaf).

Please clearly mark the boxes below to instruct your proxy how to vote.

RESOLUTIONS	FOR	AGAINST
1. To receive the report and accounts	☐	☐
2. To change the company's name to _____Limited	☐	☐

Signature(s) _____ (see note 4 overleaf)

Date _____

See all/other notes overleaf

1.19 | Proxy form (cont)

Notes:

1.   If you wish to appoint as a proxy someone other than the chairman of the meeting, please delete the words 'the chairman of the meeting' and insert the name of the other person (who need not be a member of the company). All alterations made to the proxy form must be initialled by the signatory.

2.   The completion and return of the proxy form will not prevent you from attending the AGM and voting in person should you subsequently decide to do so.

3.   If you wish your proxy to cast all of your votes for or against a resolution, you should insert an 'x' in the appropriate box. If you wish your proxy to cast only some votes for and some against, insert the relevant number of shares in the appropriate box. In the absence of instructions your proxy may vote or abstain from voting as he thinks fit on the specified resolutions, and, unless instructed otherwise, may also vote or abstain from voting as he thinks fit on any other business (including a resolution to amend a resolution, to propose a new resolution or to adjourn the meeting) which may properly come before the meeting.

4.   The proxy form must be signed by the shareholder or his attorney. Where the shareholder is a corporation the signature must be under seal or that of a duly authorised representation. In the case of joint holders, any one may sign the form. The vote of the senior joint holder (whether in person or by proxy) will be taken to the exclusion of all others, seniority being determined by the order in which the names appear in the register of members for the joint shareholding.

5.   To be valid, this proxy form and any power of attorney or other authority under which it is signed, or a certified copy of such authority, must be deposited at the company's registered office [*insert address*] no later than 48 hours before the time of the AGM or any adjournment.

1.20 | Resolution appointing corporate representative

I certify the following to be a true and correct copy of a resolution passed at a meeting of the directors of _____ Limited held on _____.

It was resolved:

THAT, in accordance with the provisions of s323 of the Companies Act 2006 _____ [*insert name 1*], and if failing him then_____ [*insert another name*], be appointed as the company's representative to act for the company at all meetings of members/creditors* of _____ Limited, and to exercise the same powers on behalf of this company as it could exercise if it were an individual shareholder/creditor/debenture holder* of the said first-named company.

Signed _____

Secretary

*Delete where inappropriate

1.21 | Notice/Agenda for Annual General Meeting

_____Limited

Notice of Annual General Meeting

Notice is given that the Annual General Meeting of the above-named company will be held at

_____ [*time*]

on   _____ [*date*]

at   _____ [*place*]

to consider the following resolutions of which resolution 1 will be proposed as an ordinary resolution and resolution 2 as a special resolution.

1.   To receive the report and accounts for the year/period ended 31 March 20_____.

2.   To resolve:

    That the name of the company be changed to _____ Limited.

A member entitled to attend the meeting is entitled to appoint one or more persons as his proxy/ies. A proxy need not be a member of the company.

On behalf of the board [*print name*] _____

Company Secretary

Date _____

Registered office (for correspondence) _____

Notes:

A form of proxy is enclosed with this notice of meeting. If you are unable to attend the meeting but still wish to vote, please complete the form of proxy and return it to _____ [name of company secretary] at _____ [registered office address] so as to arrive no later than 48 hours before the meeting.

1.22 | Letter sending out accounts and AGM notice to shareholders

This letter should be reproduced on company-headed notepaper.

To the shareholders [*names and addresses*]

Date_____

Dear Member

I have pleasure in enclosing the agenda for the forthcoming Annual General Meeting and the audited accounts of the company for the year ended _____.

Should you have any queries concerning these accounts please address them to the chairman at the above address.

I am also enclosing the notice of the Annual General Meeting and a proxy form for you to complete and return if you are unable to attend the meeting [*delete if no AGM is to be held*].

Yours faithfully

_____[*Signature*]

Secretary

1.23 | Wording for special notice

[*Address of shareholder giving notice*]

To   The directors

_____[*Name of company*]

_____[*Registered office address*]

Dear Sirs

I give notice under section 312 of the Companies Act 2006, of my intention to propose the following ordinary resolution at the Annual/Extraordinary General Meeting of the company:

RESOLUTION

[*Insert wording of resolution*]

Yours faithfully

_____

[*Signature and name of shareholder*]

1.24 | Notice of/Agenda for General Meeting

_____ Limited

Notice of general meeting

Notice is given that a general meeting of _____Limited will be held

at _____[*time*]

on _____[*date*]

at _____[*place*]

to consider the following resolution which will be proposed as a special resolution.

That the name of the company be changed to _____Limited.

A member who is entitled to attend the meeting is also entitled to appoint one or more persons as his proxy/ies. A proxy need not be a member of the company.

On behalf of the board [*print name*] _____

Company secretary

Date_____

Registered office (for correspondence)_____

Notes:

A form of proxy is enclosed with this notice of meeting. If you are unable to attend the meeting but still wish to vote, please complete the form of proxy and return it to _____ [name of company secretary] at _____ [registered office address] so as to arrive no later than 48 hours before the meeting.

1.25 | Suggested agreement to short notice

_____ Limited

Agreement of members to short notice of general meeting

I/we, the undersigned, being all of (or 90 per cent of) the member(s) of the above-named company and entitled to attend and vote at the annual/general meeting of the company, convened by a notice of meeting dated the _____ day of _____ 20_____ and to be held on the _____ day of_____ 20____ , agree that:

The meeting shall be deemed to have been duly called, notwithstanding that shorter notice than that specified in s307(1) of the Companies Act 2006 or in the company's Articles of Association has been given.

Signed _____

Print name_____Date _____

Signed _____

Print name _____Date _____

Signed _____

Print name _____Date _____

Signed _____

Print name _____Date _____

Note:

For this agreement to be effective holders of not less than 90 per cent of the issued share capital must sign. They do not all need to sign the same piece of paper.

1.26 | Typical minutes of Annual General Meeting

_____ Limited

Minutes of Annual General Meeting held on _____[date]

at _____[place]

Present _____(in the chair)

[List names of directors present] _____

_____

Company secretary _____

any other officers[e.g. auditor] _____

In addition _____ [number] members were present in person or by proxy.
[Note: There is no need to list the names of all the members present.]

1. The chairman declared the meeting open at _____ [time].

2. Notice of meeting.

   With the consent of the meeting, the notice of meeting was taken as read.

3. Report and accounts.

   It was resolved that the report and accounts for the year to 31 March 20__ be received.

4. Resolution on change of name. The special resolution on change of name to
   _____Ltd was approved by a majority of over 75 per cent and the secretary
   was instructed to submit form NM01 within 15 days to Companies House.

There being no other business to consider the meeting ended at _____ [time].

_____

Chairman

1.27a | Resolution to be filed at Companies House

COMPANIES ACT 2006
SPECIAL RESOLUTION

Company number _____

Existing company name _____

At an Annual General Meeting*/general meeting* of the members of the above named company, duly convened and held:

On the _____ day of _____ 20_____

It was resolved that [e.g. 'the name of the company be changed to

New name: _____']

Signed: _____

*Director/secretary/Community Interest Company manager (if appropriate)/administrator/ administrative receiver/receiver manager/receiver, on behalf of the company.

Notes:

- This form is for use by PLCs or private companies which choose to hold Annual General Meetings or general meetings for the purpose of a special resolution.

- A copy of the resolution must be delivered to Companies House within 15 days of its being passed.

- A fee of £10 is required to change the name (cheques made payable to 'Companies House').

- Check whether the name is available at www.companieshouse.gov.uk.

- Please provide the name and address to which the certificate is to be sent.

*delete as appropriate

1.27b | Resolution to be filed at Companies House

COMPANIES ACT 2006
WRITTEN SPECIAL RESOLUTION

Company number _____

Existing company name _____

The following special written resolution [*e.g.* 'to change the name of the company'] was agreed and passed by the members.

On the _____ day of _____ 20_____

['That the name of the company be changed to:

New name _____']

Signed _____

*Director/secretary/Community Interest Company manager (if appropriate)/administrator/ administrative receiver/receiver manager/receiver, on behalf of the company.

delete as appropriate

Notes:

- Only a private company can pass a written resolution.

- A copy of the resolution must be delivered to Companies House within 15 days of its being passed.

- A fee, currently of £10, is required to change the name (cheques made payable to 'Companies House').

- Check whether the name is available at www.companieshouse.gov.uk.

- Where applicable, please provide the name and address to which the certificate is to be sent.

- Written resolutions require a 51% majority voting in favour.

- Members have one vote per share held.

- Please refer to page 48 for further information regarding written resolutions.

1.28 | Typical board meeting agenda

The agenda must be circulated to all directors in good time before the meeting. A week beforehand is a good guide.

_____ Limited

AGENDA for BOARD MEETING to be held

At_____ [*time*]

on_____ [*date*]

at _____ [*place*]

1. Attendance/apologies for absence.

2. Minutes of the previous meeting – to be signed by the chairman.

3. Matters arising.

4. Managing director's report.

5. Financial report.

6. Consider transfer of shares.

7. Approval of director's report and accounts.

8. Any other matters raised with chairman or secretary in good time before the meeting.

Notes:

It is the secretary's duty to take notes of proceedings and write up the minutes soon afterwards. Minutes must be accurate and easily understood, not too detailed and should record who was present. They should be kept in a book or loose-leaf folder at the registered office and directors may ask to see them. If they are kept in a loose-leaf folder, the company should take adequate precautions to make sure they are not tampered with. Many companies keep their minute books in a locked cupboard.

Under the Companies Act 2006, minutes of directors' meetings should be kept for ten years.

1.29 | Contents of statutory books

This is the suggested layout for the front (introductory) sheet for the A4 file containing the statutory records (e.g. the statutory registers, etc.).

_____Ltd

STATUTORY BOOKS FILE – CONTENTS

Under Tab

1. Statutory documents
    a. Memorandum
    b. Articles of Association
    c. Certificate of Incorporation
    d. Certificate on change of name
2. Registers
    a. Applications and allotments of shares
    b. Shareholders (members)
    c. Transfers
    d. Directors
    e. Secretaries
    f. Directors' interests
    g. Charges
    h. Seals
    i. Debenture holders
3. Minutes of shareholders' meetings
4. Minutes of board meetings
5. Resolutions (signed copies)
6. Annual Returns (copies)
7. Copies of forms lodged at Companies House
8. Statutory accounts (signed copies)
9. Share transfers
    a. Forms and transfers executed
    b. Blank transfer forms
    c. Blank share certificates
    d. Cancelled share certificates
10. Contracts and deeds
    a. Directors' service contracts
    b. Shareholders' agreements
    c. Other contracts, leases and deeds

1.30a | Applications and allotments of shares

Number	Date of application	Name	Address	Description	Number of shares applied for	Amount of deposit	Distinctive numbers, if any, of shares:	Total amount in respect of shares from... to...	Further amount repayable	Amount returnable	Page in register of shareholders	Notes
1.												
2.												
3.												
4.												
5.												
6.												
7.												
8.												
9.												
10.												

1.30b | Register of Shareholders (members)

Dividends to _____

Class of share _____ Denomination _____

Disposals	Balance	Remarks

Name _____
Address _____

Date of entry as shareholder _____ Date of cessation of membership _____

Date of allotment OR Entry of transfer	References in register		Number of shares	No of Share Certificate	Amount paid or agreed to be considered as paid	Acquisitions
	Allotments	Transfers				

Dividends to _____

Class of share _____ Denomination _____

Disposals	Balance	Remarks

Name _____
Address _____

Date of entry as shareholder _____ Date of cessation of membership _____

Date of allotment OR Entry of transfer	References in register		Number of shares	No of Share Certificate	Amount paid or agreed to be considered as paid	Acquisitions
	Allotments	Transfers				

1.30c | Transfers

Transfer number	Date	Transferor's name	Address	Page in register of shareholders	Number of shares transferred	Distinctive numbers, if any, of shares from... to...	Transferee's name	Address	Page in register of shareholders	Number of shares transferred	Distinctive numbers, if any, of shares from... to...	Transfer value
1.												
2.												
3.												
4.												
5.												
6.												
7.												
8.												
9.												
10.												

1.30d | Register of Directors

The three register blocks each contain the following fields:

Surname (or corporate name)
Forename(s)
Any former forename(s) or surname(s)

Nationality _____ Date of birth _____
Residential address (or registered or principal office) _____

Other directorships _____

Business occupation _____
Date of appointment _____ minute _____
Date of filing particulars _____
Date of resignation or cessation _____ minute _____
Date of filing particulars _____

Date of resignation _____

Residential address (or registered or principal office)

Date of resignation or cessation _____ minute

Date of filing particulars

Residential address (or registered or principal office)

Date of resignation or cessation _____ minute

Date of filing particulars

Residential address (or registered or principal office)

Date of resignation or cessation _____ minute

Date of filing particulars

Residential address (or registered or principal office)

Date of resignation or cessation _____ minute

Date of filing particulars

Surname (or corporate name)

Forename(s)

Any former forename(s) or surname(s)

Date of appointment _____ minute

Date of filing particulars

Surname (or corporate name)

Forename(s)

Any former forename(s) or surname(s)

Date of appointment _____ minute

Date of filing particulars

Surname (or corporate name)

Forename(s)

Any former forename(s) or surname(s)

Date of appointment _____ minute

Date of filing particulars

Surname (or corporate name)

Forename(s)

Any former forename(s) or surname(s)

Date of appointment _____ minute

Date of filing particulars

Surname (or corporate name)

Forename(s)

Any former forename(s) or surname(s)

Date of appointment _____ minute

Date of filing particulars

1.30f | Register of Directors' Interests

Classes of share capital or debentures
(a)
(b)

Name and address of person interested

Entry		Date of		Nature of event	No of shares involved		No of shares in which interested after event	Price consideration	Remarks
No	Date	Event	Notification		Acquisitions	Disposals			

Classes of share capital or debentures
(a)
(b)

Name and address of person interested

Entry		Date of		Nature of event	No of shares involved		No of shares in which interested after event	Price consideration	Remarks
No	Date	Event	Notification		Acquisitions	Disposals			

1.30g | Register of Charges

Date	Description of instrument creating charge	Amount of charge	Rate of interest	Description of property charged	Name and address of mortgagee or person entitled to charge	Date of discharge of charge	Notes

1.30h | Debenture holders

Debenture number	Date	Amount	Description of property charged	Debenture holder's name	Address	Annual interest rate	Half-year's interest	Date interest due	Notes

1.30i | Directors' residential addresses

Name of director	Residential address
_____	_____
	_____
	_____
	_____
_____	_____
	_____
	_____
	_____
_____	_____
	_____
	_____
	_____
_____	_____
	_____
	_____
	_____
_____	_____
	_____
	_____
	_____
_____	_____
	_____
	_____
	_____

1.30j | Register of seals

Entry no	Document sealed	Date of resolution authorising seal	Date of sealing	Sealed in the presence of	Witnessed by	Where sealed document was sent

1.31 | Appointing a director

To appoint a director the board simply pass the following resolution: 'That X be appointed a director of the company with effect from _____ day of _____ 20 __ . That the secretary be instructed to make the appropriate entries in the register of directors and that form AP01 be submitted to Companies House'.

Having appointed a director it would be as well for the company secretary to write to the new director as follows:

Dear _____

At the board meeting held on _____ day of _____ 20__ you were appointed a director of this company with effect from _____ day of _____ 20__ .
I enclose form AP01 and I would be grateful if you would complete and sign it where indicated and return to me as soon as possible.

Your duties will be as follows:

*   To attend board meetings.

*   To attend general meetings of shareholders.

*   To carry out the following duties for the company   _____

_____.

Your remuneration has been agreed at £_____ and, to begin with, you will be subject to a three-month trial period. If this period proves satisfactory, your appointment will continue either indefinitely or until we agree otherwise.

I enclose a standard contract of employment which sets out your rights and responsibilities. If you have any queries, please let me know.

I also enclose a set of our latest annual/management accounts so you can see the shape this company is in.

The board welcomes you as a director and we all look forward to working with you.

Yours sincerely

_____

1.32 | Director's resignation letter

Dear Sir

I hereby resign/retire from the above company with effect from _____ day of _____ 20__.

I wish to raise the following points in connection with my departure:

• _____

• _____

I confirm that I have no outstanding claims against the company.

Yours faithfully

_____

When this happens the directors should formally minute the event as follows:

'It was noted that X had resigned/retired as director with effect from _____ day of _____ 20__. He raised the following matters in connection with his departure_____

_____.

The secretary was instructed to submit form TM01.'

In other words form TM01 must be submitted as soon as possible and within 14 days.

1.33 | Procedure for when a secretary resigns

The secretary should write to the board and his letter may simply say:

'Dear members of the board of _____Ltd,

I hereby resign as company secretary with effect from _____ day of _____ 20__.'

The directors may note the receipt of this letter by means of a board minute which might read:

'We note that X has resigned as company secretary with effect from _____ day of _____ 20__. Y has been appointed to act in his place and he was instructed to submit the necessary form(s) to Companies House.'

1.34 | Transferring shares

How do I transfer shares from one holder to another?

i. First of all, you will need to ensure that the person to whom you wish to transfer the shares has the board's approval. You may need to watch out for pre-emption rights, which means another person (existing shareholder or anyone else) has the right to buy these shares.

ii. Before you transfer shares in a limited company that you are selling, it would be as well to get the buyer and seller to sign an agreement as to what is to happen. A suggested form of agreement (contract) is included at form 1.35.

iii. Once the name of the transferee has been agreed, get a blank stock transfer form, available from Lawpack.

iv. Complete the stock transfer form as far as you (company secretary) are able and send it to the person transferring the shares (the transferor), who should send it to the company secretary with his old share certificate for it to be cancelled.

v. Send the transfer form to the transferee for him to complete his section before returning the form to the company secretary.

vi. The transfer form should be stamped, normally at the rate of £0.05p per pound of the value being transferred. The transfer may be exempt if no money is being paid for the shares. It is the purchaser of the shares that has to pay the Stamp Duty.

The address for paying Stamp Duty is:

Birmingham Stamp Office
Ninth floor
City Centre House
30 Union Street
Birmingham B2 4AR
Tel: 0845 603 0135

vii. Once this has been completed, the company secretary should note the transfer in the register of transfers, issue the new share certificate in the name of the new owner and enter his details in the shareholders' register.

viii. If the transferor is transferring only some of his shares, when you reach procedure iv above, the company secretary will issue not one but two share certificates. He will send one to the transferor for the balance of shares that he is retaining and one to the new holder for the shares he is acquiring.

ix. If the transferor is transferring his shares to more than one shareholder, separate transfer forms will be required and both will need to be stamped.

The transfer will need to be noted on the next Annual Return submitted to Companies House.

1.35 | Contract for sale of shares in a private company

Name of company _____

Offer for shares

I, _____ (vendor), offer _____ (purchaser),

the sum of £ _____ for his partial/total shareholding of

_____ ordinary shares of _____ each.

_____

Signed

_____

Dated

Acceptance of shares

I, _____ (purchaser) hereby accept the above offer and have

signed a stock transfer form to this effect on _____ [date].

_____

Signed

_____

Date

Sample documents

Company having a share capital

Memorandum of Association

of_____

Each subscriber to this Memorandum of Association wishes to form a limited company under the Companies Act 2006 and agrees to become a member of the company and to take at least one share.

Name of each subscriber   Signature   Date

2.2 | Model Articles

SCHEDULE 1 Regulation 2

MODEL ARTICLES FOR PRIVATE COMPANIES LIMITED BY SHARES

INDEX TO THE ARTICLES

2.2 | Model Articles (cont)

PART 3

SHARES AND DISTRIBUTIONS

SHARES

21. All shares to be fully paid up
22. Powers to issue different classes of share
23. Company not bound by less than absolute interests
24. Share certificates
25. Replacement share certificates
26. Share transfers
27. Transmission of shares
28. Exercise of transmittees' rights
29. Transmittees bound by prior notices

DIVIDENDS AND OTHER DISTRIBUTIONS

30. Procedure for declaring dividends
31. Payment of dividends and other distributions
32. No interest on distributions
33. Unclaimed distributions
34. Non-cash distributions
35. Waiver of distributions

CAPITALISATION OF PROFITS

36. Authority to capitalise and appropriation of capitalised sums

PART 4

DECISION-MAKING BY SHAREHOLDERS

ORGANISATION OF GENERAL MEETINGS

37. Attendance and speaking at general meetings
38. Quorum for general meetings
39. Chairing general meetings
40. Attendance and speaking by directors and non-shareholders
41. Adjournment

VOTING AT GENERAL MEETINGS

42. Voting: general
43. Errors and disputes
44. Poll votes
45. Content of proxy notices
46. Delivery of proxy notices
47. Amendments to resolutions

2.2 | Model Articles (cont)

PART 5
ADMINISTRATIVE ARRANGEMENTS

48. Means of communication to be used
49. Company seals
50. No right to inspect accounts and other records
51. Provision for employees on cessation of business

DIRECTORS' INDEMNITY AND INSURANCE

52. Indemnity
53. Insurance

PART 1
INTERPRETATION AND LIMITATION OF LIABILITY

Defined terms

1.   In the Articles, unless the context requires otherwise—

'Articles' means the company's Articles of Association;

'bankruptcy' includes individual insolvency proceedings in a jurisdiction other than England and Wales or Northern Ireland which have an effect similar to that of bankruptcy;

'chairman' has the meaning given in Article 12;

'chairman of the meeting' has the meaning given in Article 39;

'Companies Acts' means the Companies Acts (as defined in section 2 of the Companies Act 2006), in so far as they apply to the company;

'director' means a director of the company, and includes any person occupying the position of director, by whatever name called;

'distribution recipient' has the meaning given in Article 31;

'document' includes, unless otherwise specified, any document sent or supplied in electronic form;

'electronic form' has the meaning given in section 1168 of the Companies Act 2006;

'fully paid' in relation to a share, means that the nominal value and any premium to be paid to the company in respect of that share have been paid to the company;

'hard copy form' has the meaning given in section 1168 of the Companies Act 2006;

'holder' in relation to shares means the person whose name is entered in the register of members as the holder of the shares;

2.2 | Model Articles (cont)

'instrument' means a document in hard copy form;

'ordinary resolution' has the meaning given in section 282 of the Companies Act 2006;

'paid' means paid or credited as paid;

'participate', in relation to a directors' meeting, has the meaning given in Article 10;

'proxy notice' has the meaning given in Article 45;

'shareholder' means a person who is the holder of a share;

'shares' means shares in the company;

'special resolution' has the meaning given in section 283 of the Companies Act 2006;

'subsidiary' has the meaning given in section 1159 of the Companies Act 2006;

'transmittee' means a person entitled to a share by reason of the death or bankruptcy of ashareholder or otherwise by operation of law; and

'writing' means the representation or reproduction of words, symbols or other information in a visible form by any method or combination of methods, whether sent or supplied in electronic form or otherwise.

Unless the context otherwise requires, other words or expressions contained in these Articles bear the same meaning as in the Companies Act 2006 as in force on the date when these Articles become binding on the company.

Liability of members

2. The liability of the members is limited to the amount, if any, unpaid on the shares held by them.

PART 2
DIRECTORS
DIRECTORS' POWERS AND RESPONSIBILITIES

Directors' general authority

3. Subject to the Articles, the directors are responsible for the management of the company's business, for which purpose they may exercise all the powers of the company.

Shareholders' reserve power

4. 1) The shareholders may, by special resolution, direct the directors to take, or refrain from taking, specified action.

   2) No such special resolution invalidates anything which the directors have done before the passing of the resolution.

2.2 | Model Articles (cont)

Directors may delegate

5. 1) Subject to the Articles, the directors may delegate any of the powers which are conferred on them under the Articles—

    a) to such person or committee;

    b) by such means (including by power of attorney);

    c) to such an extent;

    d) in relation to such matters or territories; and

    e) on such terms and conditions;

as they think fit.

    2) If the directors so specify, any such delegation may authorise further delegation of the directors' powers by any person to whom they are delegated.

    3) The directors may revoke any delegation in whole or part, or alter its terms and conditions.

Committees

6. 1) Committees to which the directors delegate any of their powers must follow procedures which are based as far as they are applicable on those provisions of the Articles which govern the taking of decisions by directors.

    2) The directors may make rules of procedure for all or any committees, which prevail over rules derived from the Articles if they are not consistent with them.

DECISION-MAKING BY DIRECTORS

Directors to take decisions collectively

7. 1) The general rule about decision-making by directors is that any decision of the directors must be either a majority decision at a meeting or a decision taken in accordance with Article 8.

    2) If

    a) the company only has one director; and

    b) no provision of the Articles requires it to have more than one director;

the general rule does not apply, and the director may take decisions without regard to any of the provisions of the Articles relating to directors' decision-making.

2.2 | Model Articles (cont)

Unanimous decisions

8. 1) A decision of the directors is taken in accordance with this Article when all eligible directors indicate to each other by any means that they share a common view on a matter.

    2) Such a decision may take the form of a resolution in writing, copies of which have been signed by each eligible director or to which each eligible director has otherwise indicated agreement in writing.

    3) References in this Article to eligible directors are to directors who would have been entitled to vote on the matter had it been proposed as a resolution at a directors' meeting.

    4) A decision may not be taken in accordance with this Article if the eligible directors would not have formed a quorum at such a meeting.

Calling a directors' meeting

9. 1) Any director may call a directors' meeting by giving notice of the meeting to the directors or by authorising the company secretary (if any) to give such notice.

    2) Notice of any directors' meeting must indicate—

       a) its proposed date and time;

       b) where it is to take place; and

       c) if it is anticipated that directors participating in the meeting will not be in the same place, how it is proposed that they should communicate with each other during the meeting.

    3) Notice of a directors' meeting must be given to each director, but need not be in writing.

    4) Notice of a directors' meeting need not be given to directors who waive their entitlement to notice of that meeting, by giving notice to that effect to the company not more than seven days after the date on which the meeting is held. Where such notice is given after the meeting has been held, that does not affect the validity of the meeting, or of any business conducted at it.

Participation in directors' meetings

10. 1) Subject to the Articles, directors participate in a directors' meeting, or part of a directors' meeting, when—

       a) the meeting has been called and takes place in accordance with the Articles; and

    b)   they can each communicate to the others any information or opinions they have on any particular item of the business of the meeting.

2) In determining whether directors are participating in a directors' meeting, it is irrelevant where any director is or how they communicate with each other.

3) If all the directors participating in a meeting are not in the same place, they may decide that the meeting is to be treated as taking place wherever any of them is.

Quorum for directors' meetings

11. 1) At a directors' meeting, unless a quorum is participating, no proposal is to be voted on, except a proposal to call another meeting.

2) The quorum for directors' meetings may be fixed from time to time by a decision of the directors, but it must never be fewer than two, and unless otherwise fixed it is two.

3) If the total number of directors for the time being is less than the quorum required, the directors must not take any decision other than a decision to—

    a)   appoint further directors, or

    b)   call a general meeting so as to enable the shareholders to appoint further directors.

Chairing of directors' meetings

12. 1) The directors may appoint a director to chair their meetings.

2) The person so appointed for the time being is known as the chairman.

3) The directors may terminate the chairman's appointment at any time.

4) If the chairman is not participating in a directors' meeting within ten minutes of the time at which it was to start, the participating directors must appoint one of themselves to chair it.

Casting vote

13. 1) If the numbers of votes for and against a proposal are equal, the chairman or other director chairing the meeting has a casting vote.

2) But this does not apply if, in accordance with the Articles, the chairman or other director is not to be counted as participating in the decision-making process for quorum or voting purposes.

2.2 | Model Articles (cont)

Conflicts of interest

14. 1) If a proposed decision of the directors is concerned with an actual or proposed transaction or arrangement with the company in which a director is interested, that director is not to be counted as participating in the decision-making process for quorum or voting purposes.

2) But if paragraph (3) applies, a director who is interested in an actual or proposed transaction or arrangement with the company is to be counted as participating in the decision-making process for quorum and voting purposes.

3) This paragraph applies when—

   a) the company by ordinary resolution disapplies the provision of the Articles which would otherwise prevent a director from being counted as participating in the decision-making process;

   b) the director's interest cannot reasonably be regarded as likely to give rise to a conflict of interest; or

   c) the director's conflict of interest arises from a permitted cause.

4) For the purposes of this Article, the following are permitted causes—

   a) a guarantee given, or to be given, by or to a director in respect of an obligation incurred by or on behalf of the company or any of its subsidiaries;

   b) subscription, or an agreement to subscribe, for shares or other securities of the company or any of its subsidiaries, or to underwrite, sub-underwrite or guarantee subscription for any such shares or securities; and

   c) arrangements pursuant to which benefits are made available to employees and directors or former employees and directors of the company or any of its subsidiaries which do not provide special benefits for directors or former directors.

5) For the purposes of this Article, references to proposed decisions and decision-making processes include any directors' meeting or part of a directors' meeting.

6) Subject to paragraph (7), if a question arises at a meeting of directors or of a committee of directors as to the right of a director to participate in the meeting (or part of the meeting) for voting or quorum purposes, the question may, before the conclusion of the meeting, be referred to the chairman whose ruling in relation to any director other than the chairman is to be final and conclusive.

7) If any question as to the right to participate in the meeting (or part of the meeting) should arise in respect of the chairman, the question is to be decided by a decision of the directors at that meeting, for which purpose the chairman is not to be counted as participating in the meeting (or that part of the meeting) for voting or quorum purposes.

2.2 | Model Articles (cont)

Records of decisions to be kept

15. The directors must ensure that the company keeps a record, in writing, for at least ten years from the date of the decision recorded, of every unanimous or majority decision taken by the directors.

Directors' discretion to make further rules

16. Subject to the Articles, the directors may make any rule which they think fit about how they take decisions, and about how such rules are to be recorded or communicated to directors.

APPOINTMENT OF DIRECTORS

Methods of appointing directors

17. 1) Any person who is willing to act as a director, and is permitted by law to do so, may be appointed to be a director by—

   a) ordinary resolution, or

   b) a decision of the directors.

   2) In any case where, as a result of death, the company has no shareholders and no directors, the personal representatives of the last shareholder to have died have the right, by notice in writing, to appoint a person to be a director.

   3) For the purposes of paragraph (2), where two or more shareholders die in circumstances rendering it uncertain who was the last to die, a younger shareholder is deemed to have survived an older shareholder.

Termination of director's appointment

18. A person ceases to be a director as soon as—

   a) that person ceases to be a director by virtue of any provision of the Companies Act 2006 or is prohibited from being a director by law;

   b) a bankruptcy order is made against that person;

   c) a composition is made with that person's creditors generally in satisfaction of that person's debts;

   d) a registered medical practitioner who is treating that person gives a written opinion to the company stating that that person has become physically or mentally incapable of acting as a director and may remain so for more than three months;

   e) by reason of that person's mental health, a court makes an order which wholly or partly prevents that person from personally exercising any powers or rights which that person would otherwise have;

f)   notification is received by the company from the director that the director is resigning from office, and such resignation has taken effect in accordance with its terms.

Directors' remuneration

19.   1)   Directors may undertake any services for the company that the directors decide.

2)   Directors are entitled to such remuneration as the directors determine for —

   a)   their services to the company as directors, and

   b)   any other service which they undertake for the company.

3)   Subject to the Articles, a director's remuneration may—

   a)   take any form; and

   b)   include any arrangements in connection with the payment of a pension, allowance or gratuity, or any death, sickness or disability benefits, to or in respect of that director.

4)   Unless the directors decide otherwise, directors' remuneration accrues from day to day.

5)   Unless the directors decide otherwise, directors are not accountable to the company for any remuneration which they receive as directors or other officers or employees of the company's subsidiaries or of any other body corporate in which the company is interested.

Directors' expenses

20.   The company may pay any reasonable expenses which the directors properly incur in connection with their attendance at—

a)   meetings of directors or committees of directors;

b)   general meetings; or

c)   separate meetings of the holders of any class of shares or of debentures of the company, or otherwise in connection with the exercise of their powers and the discharge of their responsibilities in relation to the company.

PART 3
SHARES AND DISTRIBUTIONS
SHARES

All shares to be fully paid up

21. 1) No share is to be issued for less than the aggregate of its nominal value and any premium to be paid to the company in consideration for its issue.

2) This does not apply to shares taken on the formation of the company by the subscribers to the company's Memorandum.

Powers to issue different classes of share

22. 1) Subject to the Articles, but without prejudice to the rights attached to any existing share, the company may issue shares with such rights or restrictions as may be determined by ordinary resolution.

2) The company may issue shares which are to be redeemed, or are liable to be redeemed at the option of the company or the holder, and the directors may determine the terms, conditions and manner of redemption of any such shares.

Company not bound by less than absolute interests

23. Except as required by law, no person is to be recognised by the company as holding any share upon any trust, and except as otherwise required by law or the Articles, the company is not in any way to be bound by or recognise any interest in a share other than the holder's absolute ownership of it and all the rights attaching to it.

Share certificates

24. 1) The company must issue each shareholder, free of charge, with one or more certificates in respect of the shares which that shareholder holds.

2) Every certificate must specify—

   a) in respect of how many shares, of what class, it is issued;

   b) the nominal value of those shares;

   c) that the shares are fully paid; and

   d) any distinguishing numbers assigned to them.

3) No certificate may be issued in respect of shares of more than one class.

4) If more than one person holds a share, only one certificate may be issued in respect of it.

5) Certificates must—

   a) have affixed to them the company's common seal; or

   b) be otherwise executed in accordance with the Companies Acts.

2.2 | Model Articles (cont)

Replacement share certificates

25. 1) If a certificate issued in respect of a shareholder's shares is—

    a) damaged or defaced; or

    b) said to be lost, stolen or destroyed, that shareholder is entitled to a replacement certificate in respect of the same shares.

  2) A shareholder exercising the right to be issued with such a replacement certificate—

    a) may at the same time exercise the right to be issued with a single certificate or separate certificates;

    b) must return the certificate which is to be replaced to the company if it is damaged or defaced; and

    c) must comply with such conditions as to evidence, indemnity and the payment of a reasonable fee as the directors decide.

Share transfers

26. 1) Shares may be transferred by means of an instrument of transfer in any usual form or any other form approved by the directors, which is executed by or on behalf of the transferor.

  2) No fee may be charged for registering any instrument of transfer or other document relating to or affecting the title to any share.

  3) The company may retain any instrument of transfer which is registered.

  4) The transferor remains the holder of a share until the transferee's name is entered in the register of members as holder of it.

  5) The directors may refuse to register the transfer of a share, and if they do so, the instrument of transfer must be returned to the transferee with the notice of refusal unless they suspect that the proposed transfer may be fraudulent.

Transmission of shares

27. 1) If title to a share passes to a transmittee, the company may only recognise the transmittee as having any title to that share.

  2) A transmittee who produces such evidence of entitlement to shares as the directors may properly require—

    a) may, subject to the Articles, choose either to become the holder of those shares or to have them transferred to another person; and

b) subject to the Articles, and pending any transfer of the shares to another person, has the same rights as the holder had.

3) But transmittees do not have the right to attend or vote at a general meeting, or agree to a proposed written resolution, in respect of shares to which they are entitled, by reason of the holder's death or bankruptcy or otherwise, unless they become the holders of those shares.

Exercise of transmittees' rights

28. 1) Transmittees who wish to become the holders of shares to which they have become entitled must notify the company in writing of that wish.

2) If the transmittee wishes to have a share transferred to another person, the transmittee must execute an instrument of transfer in respect of it.

3) Any transfer made or executed under this Article is to be treated as if it were made or executed by the person from whom the transmittee has derived rights in respect of the share, and as if the event which gave rise to the transmission had not occurred.

Transmittees bound by prior notices

29. If a notice is given to a shareholder in respect of shares and a transmittee is entitled to those shares, the transmittee is bound by the notice if it was given to the shareholder before the transmittee's name has been entered in the register of members.

DIVIDENDS AND OTHER DISTRIBUTIONS
Procedure for declaring dividends

30. 1) The company may by ordinary resolution declare dividends, and the directors may decide to pay interim dividends.

2) A dividend must not be declared unless the directors have made a recommendation as to its amount. Such a dividend must not exceed the amount recommended by the directors.

3) No dividend may be declared or paid unless it is in accordance with shareholders' respective rights.

4) Unless the shareholders' resolution to declare or directors' decision to pay a dividend, or the terms on which shares are issued, specify otherwise, it must be paid by reference to each shareholder's holding of shares on the date of the resolution or decision to declare or pay it.

5) If the company's share capital is divided into different classes, no interim dividend may be paid on shares carrying deferred or non-preferred rights if, at the time of payment, any preferential dividend is in arrear.

6) The directors may pay at intervals any dividend payable at a fixed rate if it appears to them that the profits available for distribution justify the payment.

7) If the directors act in good faith, they do not incur any liability to the holders of shares conferring preferred rights for any loss they may suffer by the lawful payment of an interim dividend on shares with deferred or non-preferred rights.

Payment of dividends and other distributions

31. 1) Where a dividend or other sum which is a distribution is payable in respect of a share, it must be paid by one or more of the following means—

   a) transfer to a bank or building society account specified by the distribution recipient either in writing or as the directors may otherwise decide;

   b) sending a cheque made payable to the distribution recipient by post to the distribution recipient at the distribution recipient's registered address (if the distribution recipient is a holder of the share), or (in any other case) to an address specified by the distribution recipient either in writing or as the directors may otherwise decide;

   c) sending a cheque made payable to such person by post to such person at such address as the distribution recipient has specified either in writing or as the directors may otherwise decide; or

   d) any other means of payment as the directors agree with the distribution recipient either in writing or by such other means as the directors decide.

2) In the Articles, 'the distribution recipient' means, in respect of a share in respect of which a dividend or other sum is payable—

   a) the holder of the share; or

   b) if the share has two or more joint holders, whichever of them is named first in the register of members; or

   c) if the holder is no longer entitled to the share by reason of death or bankruptcy, or otherwise by operation of law, the transmittee.

No interest on distributions

32. The company may not pay interest on any dividend or other sum payable in respect of a share unless otherwise provided by—

   a) the terms on which the share was issued; or

   b) the provisions of another agreement between the holder of that share and the company.

Unclaimed distributions

33. 1) All dividends or other sums which are—

    a) payable in respect of shares; and

    b) unclaimed after having been declared or become payable,

may be invested or otherwise made use of by the directors for the benefit of the company until claimed.

2) The payment of any such dividend or other sum into a separate account does not make the company a trustee in respect of it.

3) If

    a) twelve years have passed from the date on which a dividend or other sum became due for payment, and

    b) the distribution recipient has not claimed it,

the distribution recipient is no longer entitled to that dividend or other sum and it ceases to remain owing by the company.

Non-cash distributions

34. 1) Subject to the terms of issue of the share in question, the company may, by ordinary resolution on the recommendation of the directors, decide to pay all or part of a dividend or other distribution payable in respect of a share by transferring non-cash assets of equivalent value (including, without limitation, shares or other securities in any company).

2) For the purposes of paying a non-cash distribution, the directors may make whatever arrangements they think fit, including, where any difficulty arises regarding the distribution—

    a) fixing the value of any assets;

    b) paying cash to any distribution recipient on the basis of that value in order to adjust the rights of recipients; and

    c) vesting any assets in trustees.

Waiver of distributions

35. Distribution recipients may waive their entitlement to a dividend or other distribution payable in respect of a share by giving the company notice in writing to that effect, but if—

    a) the share has more than one holder; or

b) more than one person is entitled to the share, whether by reason of the death or bankruptcy of one or more joint holders, or otherwise;

the notice is not effective unless it is expressed to be given, and signed, by all the holders or persons otherwise entitled to the share.

CAPITALISATION OF PROFITS
Authority to capitalise and appropriation of capitalised sums

36. 1) Subject to the Articles, the directors may, if they are so authorised by an ordinary resolution—

a) decide to capitalise any profits of the company (whether or not they are available for distribution) which are not required for paying a preferential dividend, or any sum standing to the credit of the company's share premium account or capital redemption reserve; and

b) appropriate any sum which they so decide to capitalise (a 'capitalised sum') to the persons who would have been entitled to it if it were distributed by way of dividend (the 'persons entitled') and in the same proportions.

2) Capitalised sums must be applied—

a) on behalf of the persons entitled; and

b) in the same proportions as a dividend would have been distributed to them.

3) Any capitalised sum may be applied in paying up new shares of a nominal amount equal to the capitalised sum which are then allotted credited as fully paid to the persons entitled or as they may direct.

4) A capitalised sum which was appropriated from profits available for distribution may be applied in paying up new debentures of the company which are then allotted credited as fully paid to the persons entitled or as they may direct.

5) Subject to the Articles the directors may—

a) apply capitalised sums in accordance with paragraphs (3) and (4) partly in one way and partly in another;

b) make such arrangements as they think fit to deal with shares or debentures becoming distributable in fractions under this Article (including the issuing of fractional certificates or the making of cash payments); and

c) authorise any person to enter into an agreement with the company on behalf of all the persons entitled which is binding on them in respect of the allotment of shares and debentures to them under this Article.

PART 4
DECISION-MAKING BY SHAREHOLDERS
ORGANISATION OF GENERAL MEETINGS

Attendance and speaking at general meetings

37. 1) A person is able to exercise the right to speak at a general meeting when that person is in a position to communicate to all those attending the meeting, during the meeting, any information or opinions which that person has on the business of the meeting.

    2) A person is able to exercise the right to vote at a general meeting when—

       a) that person is able to vote, during the meeting, on resolutions put to the vote at the meeting; and

       b) that person's vote can be taken into account in determining whether or not such resolutions are passed at the same time as the votes of all the other persons attending the meeting.

    3) The directors may make whatever arrangements they consider appropriate to enable those attending a general meeting to exercise their rights to speak or vote at it.

    4) In determining attendance at a general meeting, it is immaterial whether any two or more members attending it are in the same place as each other.

    5) Two or more persons who are not in the same place as each other attend a general meeting if their circumstances are such that if they have (or were to have) rights to speak and vote at that meeting, they are (or would be) able to exercise them.

Quorum for general meetings

38. No business other than the appointment of the chairman of the meeting is to be transacted at a general meeting if the persons attending it do not constitute a quorum.

Chairing general meetings

39. 1) If the directors have appointed a chairman, the chairman shall chair general meetings if present and willing to do so.

    2) If the directors have not appointed a chairman, or if the chairman is unwilling to chair the meeting or is not present within ten minutes of the time at which a meeting was due to start—

       a) the directors present; or

       b) (if no directors are present), the meeting;

       must appoint a director or shareholder to chair the meeting, and the appointment of the chairman of the meeting must be the first business of the meeting.

3) The person chairing a meeting in accordance with this Article is referred to as 'the chairman of the meeting'.

Attendance and speaking by directors and non-shareholders

40. 1) Directors may attend and speak at general meetings, whether or not they are shareholders.

2) The chairman of the meeting may permit other persons who are not—

   a) shareholders of the company; or

   b) otherwise entitled to exercise the rights of shareholders in relation to general meetings;

   to attend and speak at a general meeting.

Adjournment

41. 1) If the persons attending a general meeting within half an hour of the time at which the meeting was due to start do not constitute a quorum, or if during a meeting a quorum ceases to be present, the chairman of the meeting must adjourn it.

2) The chairman of the meeting may adjourn a general meeting at which a quorum is present if—

   a) the meeting consents to an adjournment; or

   b) it appears to the chairman of the meeting that an adjournment is necessary to protect the safety of any person attending the meeting or ensure that the business of the meeting is conducted in an orderly manner.

3) The chairman of the meeting must adjourn a general meeting if directed to do so by the meeting.

4) When adjourning a general meeting, the chairman of the meeting must—

   a) either specify the time and place to which it is adjourned or state that it is to continue at a time and place to be fixed by the directors; and

   b) have regard to any directions as to the time and place of any adjournment which have been given by the meeting.

5) If the continuation of an adjourned meeting is to take place more than 14 days after it was adjourned, the company must give at least 7 clear days' notice of it (that is, excluding the day of the adjourned meeting and the day on which the notice is given)—

   a) to the same persons to whom notice of the company's general meetings is required to be given; and

b) containing the same information which such notice is required to contain.

6) No business may be transacted at an adjourned general meeting which could not properly have been transacted at the meeting if the adjournment had not taken place.

VOTING AT GENERAL MEETINGS

Voting: general

42. A resolution put to the vote of a general meeting must be decided on a show of hands unless a poll is duly demanded in accordance with the Articles.

Errors and disputes

43. 1) No objection may be raised to the qualification of any person voting at a general meeting except at the meeting or adjourned meeting at which the vote objected to is tendered, and every vote not disallowed at the meeting is valid.

2) Any such objection must be referred to the chairman of the meeting, whose decision is final.

Poll votes

44. 1) A poll on a resolution may be demanded—

a) in advance of the general meeting where it is to be put to the vote; or

b) at a general meeting, either before a show of hands on that resolution or immediately after the result of a show of hands on that resolution is declared.

2) A poll may be demanded by—

a) the chairman of the meeting;

b) the directors;

c) two or more persons having the right to vote on the resolution; or

d) a person or persons representing not less than one-tenth of the total voting rights of all the shareholders having the right to vote on the resolution.

3) A demand for a poll may be withdrawn if—

a) the poll has not yet been taken; and

b) the chairman of the meeting consents to the withdrawal.

4) Polls must be taken immediately and in such manner as the chairman of the meeting directs.

Content of proxy notices

45. 1) Proxies may only validly be appointed by a notice in writing (a 'proxy notice') which—

    a) states the name and address of the shareholder appointing the proxy;

    b) identifies the person appointed to be that shareholder's proxy and the general meeting in relation to which that person is appointed;

    c) is signed by or on behalf of the shareholder appointing the proxy, or is authenticated in such manner as the directors may determine; and

    d) is delivered to the company in accordance with the Articles and any instructions contained in the notice of the general meeting to which they relate.

2) The company may require proxy notices to be delivered in a particular form, and may specify different forms for different purposes.

3) Proxy notices may specify how the proxy appointed under them is to vote (or that the proxy is to abstain from voting) on one or more resolutions.

4) Unless a proxy notice indicates otherwise, it must be treated as—

    a) allowing the person appointed under it as a proxy discretion as to how to vote on any ancillary or procedural resolutions put to the meeting; and

    b) appointing that person as a proxy in relation to any adjournment of the general meeting to which it relates as well as the meeting itself.

Delivery of proxy notices

46. 1) A person who is entitled to attend, speak or vote (either on a show of hands or on a poll) at a general meeting remains so entitled in respect of that meeting or any adjournment of it, even though a valid proxy notice has been delivered to the company by or on behalf of that person.

2) An appointment under a proxy notice may be revoked by delivering to the company a notice in writing given by or on behalf of the person by whom or on whose behalf the proxy notice was given.

3) A notice revoking a proxy appointment only takes effect if it is delivered before the start of the meeting or adjourned meeting to which it relates.

4) If a proxy notice is not executed by the person appointing the proxy, it must be accompanied by written evidence of the authority of the person who executed it to execute it on the appointor's behalf.

Amendments to resolutions

2.2 | Model Articles (cont)

47. 1) An ordinary resolution to be proposed at a general meeting may be amended by ordinary resolution if—

 a) notice of the proposed amendment is given to the company in writing by a person entitled to vote at the general meeting at which it is to be proposed not less than 48 hours before the meeting is to take place (or such later time as the chairman of the meeting may determine); and

 b) the proposed amendment does not, in the reasonable opinion of the chairman of the meeting, materially alter the scope of the resolution.

 2) A special resolution to be proposed at a general meeting may be amended by ordinary resolution; if—

 a) the chairman of the meeting proposes the amendment at the general meeting at which the resolution is to be proposed; and

 b) the amendment does not go beyond what is necessary to correct a grammatical or other non-substantive error in the resolution.

 3) If the chairman of the meeting, acting in good faith, wrongly decides that an amendment to a resolution is out of order, the chairman's error does not invalidate the vote on that resolution.

PART 5
ADMINISTRATIVE ARRANGEMENTS

Means of communication to be used

48. 1) Subject to the Articles, anything sent or supplied by or to the company under the Articles may be sent or supplied in any way in which the Companies Act 2006 provides for documents or information which are authorised or required by any provision of that Act to be sent or supplied by or to the company.

 2) Subject to the Articles, any notice or document to be sent or supplied to a director in connection with the taking of decisions by directors may also be sent or supplied by the means by which that director has asked to be sent or supplied with such notices or documents for the time being.

 3) A director may agree with the company that notices or documents sent to that director in a particular way are to be deemed to have been received within a specified time of their being sent, and for the specified time to be less than 48 hours.

Company seals

49. 1) Any common seal may only be used by the authority of the directors.

2) The directors may decide by what means and in what form any common seal is to be used.

3) Unless otherwise decided by the directors, if the company has a common seal and it is affixed to a document, the document must also be signed by at least one authorised person in the presence of a witness who attests the signature.

4) For the purposes of this Article, an authorised person is—

   a) any director of the company;

   b) the company secretary (if any); or

   c) any person authorised by the directors for the purpose of signing documents to which the common seal is applied.

No right to inspect accounts and other records

50. Except as provided by law or authorised by the directors or an ordinary resolution of the company, no person is entitled to inspect any of the company's accounting or other records or documents merely by virtue of being a shareholder.

Provision for employees on cessation of business

51. The directors may decide to make provision for the benefit of persons employed or formerly employed by the company or any of its subsidiaries (other than a director or former director or shadow director) in connection with the cessation or transfer to any person of the whole or part of the undertaking of the company or that subsidiary.

DIRECTORS' INDEMNITY AND INSURANCE
Indemnity

52. 1) Subject to paragraph (2), a relevant director of the company or an associated company may be indemnified out of the company's assets against—

   a) any liability incurred by that director in connection with any negligence, default, breach of duty or breach of trust in relation to the company or an associated company;

   b) any liability incurred by that director in connection with the activities of the company or an associated company in its capacity as a trustee of an occupational pension scheme (as defined in section 235(6) of the Companies Act 2006);

   c) any other liability incurred by that director as an officer of the company or an associated company.

2) This Article does not authorise any indemnity which would be prohibited or rendered void by any provision of the Companies Acts or by any other provision of law.

2.2 | Model Articles (cont)

3) In this Article—

   a) companies are associated if one is a subsidiary of the other or both are subsidiaries of the same body corporate; and

   b) a 'relevant director' means any director or former director of the company or an associated company.

Insurance

53. 1) The directors may decide to purchase and maintain insurance, at the expense of the company, for the benefit of any relevant director in respect of any relevant loss.

   2) In this article—

   a) a 'relevant director' means any director or former director of the company or an associated company;

   b) a 'relevant loss' means any loss or liability which has been or may be incurred by a relevant director in connection with that director's duties or powers in relation to the company, any associated company or any pension fund or employees' share scheme of the company or associated company; and

   c) companies are associated if one is a subsidiary of the other or both are subsidiaries of the same body corporate.

2.3 | Contents of Table A

Prior to 1 October 2009 many private companies adopted Table A of the Companies Act 1985 as their Articles of Association. Every company secretary should have a copy of the Companies Act 1985 and the Companies Act 2006, which are available through booksellers and The Stationery Office (tel: 0870 600 5522). A copy of Table A (Statutory Instrument 1985 No 805 (ISBN 978-0110568 05 8) may also be obtained from these sources. The Companies Act 2006 can be accessed via www.opsi.gov.uk.

One problem with the old Table A was that it did not come with a contents sheet and so it was often difficult finding one's way around the suggested Articles. If this is a problem you face, you will find below our own suggested contents to help you. A transitional version of Table A was also published prior to 1 October 2009 so be careful which version of Table A you are referring to.

The 1985 version of Table A covered the following areas:

	Regulations
Share capital	2–5
Share certificates	6–7
Lien	8–11
Calls on shares	12–22
Transfer of shares	23–28
Transmission of shares	29–31
Alteration of capital	32–34
Purchase of own shares	35
General meetings	36–37
Notice of general meetings	38–39
Proceedings of general meetings	40–53
Votes of members	54–63
Number of directors	64
Alternate directors	65–69
Powers of directors	70–71
Delegation of directors' powers	72
Appointment and retirement of directors	73–80
Disqualification and removal of directors	81
Remuneration of directors	82

2.3 | Contents of Table A (cont)

CERTIFICATE OF INCORPORATION
OF A PRIVATE LIMITED COMPANY

Company No. .

The Registrar of Companies for England and Wales hereby certifies that

.

is this day incorporated under the Companies Act 2006 as a private company and that the company is limited by shares, and the situation of its registered office is in ENGLAND/WALES

Given at Companies House, Cardiff, the ..

THE OFFICIAL SEAL OF THE
REGISTRAR OF COMPANIES

Companies House
—— *for the record* ——

2.5 | Share certificate

Certificate No. _____

Number of Shares _____

This is to Certify that _____

of _____

is/are the Registered holder(s) of _____ shares of £ _____ each

_____ paid in the above-named Company, subject to the Memorandum and

Articles of Association of the Company.

*This document is hereby executed by the Company /

The Common Seal of the Company was hereto affixed in the presence of:

_____
_____ Directors

_____
_____ Secretary

_____ 20 _____

* *Delete as appropriate*

2.6 | Stock transfer form

STOCK TRANSFER FORM

(Above this line for Registrars only)

Certificate lodged with the Registrar

Consideration Money £ ....

(For completion by the Registrar/Stock Exchange)

Name of Undertaking	
Description of Security	

Number or amount of Shares, Stock or other security and, in figures column only, number and denomination of units, if any.	Words	Figures
		(units of)

Names(s) of registered holder(s) should be given in full: the address should be given where there is only one holder. If the transfer is not made by the registered holder(s) insert also the name(s) and capacity (e.g. Executor(s) of the person(s) making the transfer).	In the name(s) of

I/We hereby transfer the above security out of the name(s) aforesaid to the person(s) named below.

Signature(s) of transferor(s)

1. ....

2. ....

3. ....

4. ....

A body corporate should execute this transfer under its common seal or otherwise in accordance with applicable statutory requirements.

Stamp of Selling Broker(s) or, for transactions which are not stock exchange transactions, of Agent(s), if any, acting for the Transferor(s)

Date

Full name(s) and full postal address(es) (including County or, if applicable, Postal District number) of the person(s) to whom the security is transferred.

Please state title, if any, or whether Mr., Mrs. or Miss.

Please complete in typewriting or Block Capitals.

I/We request that such entries be made in the register as are necessary to give effect to this transfer.

Stamp of Buying Broker(s) (if any)	Stamp or name and address of person lodging this form (if other than the Buying Broker(s))

Reference to the Registrar in this Form means the registrar or registration agent of the undertaking NOT the Registrar of Companies at Companies House.

2.6 | Stock transfer form (cont)

Form of certificate required where transfer is exempt from Ad Valorem stamp duty as below threshold

(1)   I/We hereby certify that the transaction effected by this instrument does not form part of a larger transaction or series of transactions in respect of which the amount or value, or aggregate amount or value, of the consideration exceeds £1000.

(1)   I/We confirm that (1) I/we have been authorised by the transferor to sign this certificate and that the facts of the transaction are
within (1) my/our knowledge (2).

(1) Delete as appropriate.
(2) Delete second sentence if certificate is given by transferor or his solicitor.

Signature(s)   Description or capacity ('Transferor', 'Solicitor', etc.)

_____   _____

_____   _____

_____   _____

_____   _____

Date _____ 20 _____

Notes:
(1) If the above certificate has been completed, this transfer does not need to be submitted to the Stamp Office but should be sent directly to the Company or its Registrars.
(2) If the above certificate has not been completed, this transfer needs to be submitted to an Inland Revenue Stamp Office and duly stamped.

APPENDIX 3
Quick cribs

Most books on company law tend to be thick and verbose. Because most users of this book want to get to a simple answer quickly, we have included the following Appendix to summarise in very easy terms how one carries out most of the usual procedures.

Quick cribs

Please be aware that Columns B, C and I are of no immediate concern to Companies House, but you are reminded of the obligation to keep all your statutory records up to date.

A	B	C	D	E	F	G	H	I
What do you want to do?	Board resolution required?	Members' meeting required?	What sort of notice?	What sort of resolution?	Majority required	Form to submit to Companies House	Fee payable?	Amendments needed to statutory books?
3.1 Change the company's name	Yes	This can be done by a written special resolution of the directors alone, but it is more usual to get shareholder approval, which can also be by written resolution	15 days	Special	75%	NM01. Note there are alternative NM forms that might need to be submitted. If the directors decide on the change, then file form Res CA 2006. You also need to file an amended copy of the Memorandum and Articles with the form	£10 or £50 for same day service	None, except that all forms and registers should show the new name

A	B	C	D	E	F	G	H	I
What do you want to do?	Board resolution required?	Members' meeting required?	What sort of notice?	What sort of resolution?	Majority required	Form to submit to Companies House	Fee payable?	Amendments needed to statutory books?
3.2 Change the Articles	Yes	Yes	15 days	Special	75%	The original signed resolution plus a copy of the new Articles	N/A	File a copy of the new Articles in the statutory books
3.3 Adopt the new Model Articles in their entirety	Yes	Yes	15 days	Special	75%	The original signed resolution	N/A	File a copy of the new Articles in the statutory books
3.4 Appoint a director	Yes	No	N/A	N/A	N/A	AP01 or AP02	N/A	Change the register of directors
3.5 Remove a director	Yes	Yes	28 days	Ordinary	51%	TM01	N/A	Change the register of directors
3.6 A director wants to resign	No. The board notes and minutes the resignation	No	N/A	N/A	N/A	TM01	N/A	Change the register of directors

A What do you want to do?	B Board resolution required?	C Members' meeting required?	D What sort of notice?	E What sort of resolution?	F Majority required	G Form to submit to Companies House	H Fee payable?	I Amendments needed to statutory books?
3.7 Appoint a secretary	Yes	No	N/A	N/A	N/A	AP03 or AP04	N/A	Change the register of secretaries
3.8 Remove a secretary	Yes	No	N/A	N/A	N/A	TM02	N/A	Change the register of secretaries
3.9 A secretary wants to resign	No. The board notes and minutes the resignation	No	N/A	N/A	N/A	TM02	N/A	Change the register of secretaries
3.10 Appoint an auditor	Yes	No	N/A	N/A	N/A	N/A	N/A	N/A
3.11 Remove an auditor	Yes	Yes	14 days	Ordinary	51%	AA03	N/A	N/A
3.12 An auditor wants to resign	No. The board notes and minutes the resignation	No	N/A	N/A	N/A	The letter of resignation from the auditor	N/A	N/A

A	B	C	D	E	F	G	H	I
What do you want to do?	**Board resolution required?**	**Members' meeting required?**	**What sort of notice?**	**What sort of resolution?**	**Majority required**	**Form to submit to Companies House**	**Fee payable?**	**Amendments needed to statutory books?**
3.13 Hold a meeting or AGM	Yes	No	N/A	N/A	N/A	N/A	N/A	N/A
3.14 Pay a dividend	Yes	No	N/A	N/A	N/A	N/A	N/A	N/A
3.15 Make a rights issue (i.e. issue more shares for cash)	Yes	No	N/A	N/A	N/A	SH01	N/A	Mark details of the new shares issued
3.16 Make a scrip or bonus issue (i.e. turn accumulated profits into shares)	Yes	Yes	14 days	Ordinary	51%	SH01	N/A	Mark details of the new shares issued
3.17 Make a call on shares	Yes	No	N/A	N/A	N/A	SH01	N/A	Mark details of sums paid in the shareholders' register

	A	B	C	D	E	F	G	H	I
	What do you want to do?	**Board resolution required?**	**Members' meeting required?**	**What sort of notice?**	**What sort of resolution?**	**Majority required**	**Form to submit to Companies House**	**Fee payable?**	**Amendments needed to statutory books?**
3.18	Vary the rights of a class of shareholders	Yes	Yes	28 days	Special	75%	SH10	N/A	File a copy of the Articles showing the variation
3.19	Transfer shares	Yes	No	N/A	N/A	N/A	N/A	N/A	Change the details in the register for both the transferor as well as the transferee
3.20	Forfeit shares (NB: There are different rules for PLCs)	Yes	No	N/A	N/A	N/A	N/A	N/A	Enter details in the shareholders' register
3.21	Create a shareholders' agreement	Yes	Yes, although the arrangements are put in place by means of them all signing the agreement	N/A	N/A	N/A	N/A	N/A	File original agreement in the statutory books

A	B	C	D	E	F	G	H	I
What do you want to do?	**Board resolution required?**	**Members' meeting required?**	**What sort of notice?**	**What sort of resolution?**	**Majority required**	**Form to submit to Companies House**	**Fee payable?**	**Amendments needed to statutory books?**
3.22 Form another company	Yes	Probably not. It would not be a requirement but it may be sensible to hold a general meeting to agree this matter	14 days	Ordinary	51%	IN01	£14 software filing £18 web filing £40 standard paper £100 same day paper	No. The new company will have its own set of statutory books
3.23 Waive a dividend	No. This would be the decision of the shareholder concerned	No	N/A	N/A	N/A	N/A	N/A	No
3.24 Pass a written resolution	Yes	Yes	This will depend on the resolution being considered					
3.25 Make private company public	Yes	Yes	15 days	Special	75%	RR01	£20	File amended Cert. of Inc.

A	B	C	D	E	F	G	H	I
What do you want to do?	**Board resolution required?**	**Members' meeting required?**	**What sort of notice?**	**What sort of resolution?**	**Majority required**	**Form to submit to Companies House**	**Fee payable?**	**Amendments needed to statutory books?**
3.26 Change the registered office	Yes	No	N/A	N/A	N/A	AD01	N/A	
3.27 Issue proxy forms	Yes	N/A	N/A	N/A	N/A	N/A	N/A	N/A
3.28 Appoint a corporate director	Yes	No	N/A	N/A	N/A	AP02	N/A	Enter details in the register of directors
3.29 Hold a board meeting	Yes	N/A	N/A	N/A	N/A	N/A	N/A	N/A
3.30 Borrow money on company security	Yes	No	N/A	N/A	N/A	MG01	£13	Enter details in the register of charges

A	B	C	D	E	F	G	H	I
What do you want to do?	Board resolution required?	Members' meeting required?	What sort of notice?	What sort of resolution?	Majority required	Form to submit to Companies House	Fee payable?	Amendments needed to statutory books?
3.31 Strike a company off (This is not the same as a 'winding-up' for which specialist professional advice must be sought)	Yes	Yes	28 days	Special	75%	DS01	£10	N/A
3.32 Change location of the company's statutory books	Yes	No	N/A	N/A	N/A	AD02, AD03 or AD04	N/A	N/A

APPENDIX 4

Common Companies House Forms

New no	Purpose	Old no (Pre-01/10/09)
AA01	Change of accounting reference date	225
AA03	Notice of resolution removing auditors from office	391
AD01	Change of registered office address	287
AD02	Notification of single alternative inspection location (SAIL) for the company's statutory books	353
AD03	Change of location of the company's records (statutory books) to the single alternative inspection location	325
AD04	Change of location of the company's records (statutory books) to the registered office	325
AP01	Appointment of director	288a
AP02	Appointment of corporate director	288a
AP03	Appointment of secretary	288a
AR01	Annual Return	363
CH01	Change of director's details	288c
CH03	Change of secretary's details	288c
DS01	Application for striking off	652a
IN01	Application to register a company	10 and 12
MG01	Particulars of mortgage or charge	395
MG02	Statement of satisfaction in full or in part of mortgage or charge	403a
NM02	Notice of change of name by conditional resolution	N/A
NM03	Notice confirming satisfaction of the conditional resolution for change of name	N/A

New no	Purpose	Old no (Pre-01/10/09)
NM04	Notice of change of name by means provided for in the Articles	N/A
NM05	Notice of change of name by resolution of directors	N/A
NM06	Request to seek comments of government department or other specified body on change of name	N/A
Res CA 2006	Special resolution on change of name	N/A
Written Res CA 2006	Written special resolution on change of name	N/A
SH01	Return of allotment of shares	88(2)
SH03	Return of purchase of own shares	169
SH06	Notice of cancellation of shares	N/A
SH08	Notice of name or other designation of class of shares	128(4)
SH10	Notice of particulars of variation of rights attached to shares	128(3)
TM01	Termination of appointment of director	288b
TM02	Termination of appointment of secretary	288b

Glossary

accounting reference date – the annual anniversary upon which a company's financial year ends.

accounting reference period – the period which ends on the accounting reference date.

administration order – the order of a court to appoint an administrator to manage a company in financial difficulties in an attempt to secure its survival or winding–up.

allotment – the appropriation of shares in the capital of the company to the applicants for those shares, by the board.

Annual General Meeting (AGM) – is no longer obligatory, but are still a good idea. Annual meetings of a company's shareholders to lay the annual accounts and directors' and auditors' reports before the shareholders and deal with other matters. Private companies can dispense with the need for AGMs by passing resolutions.

Annual Return – a prescribed form which must be filed annually with Companies House by a limited company, detailing the company's activities for the period up to the anniversary of the company's incorporation.

Articles of Association (or 'Articles') – the document containing the company's regulations for its internal management.

asset – anything owned with monetary value. This includes both real and personal property.

auditor – a person appointed to examine the accounts of a registered company and to report on them to company members.

authorised capital – this was the nominal capital which the company was authorised to issue by its Memorandum of Association. The concept of authorised capital has been abolished by the Companies Act 2006.

board – the directors of a company.

board meeting – a meeting of the directors.

company seal – a company may execute deeds by affixing its seal to them. There is no longer any requirement for a company to have a seal and it may execute deeds by either two directors or a director and the company secretary signing the relevant document.

director – an officer of the company who manages company business and has a duty of care, skill and good faith.

elective resolution – a resolution which a private company was entitled to pass to reduce or remove certain administrative or formal requirements. It required the consent of all those shareholders entitled to vote. These no longer apply since the introduction of the Companies Act 2006.

Extraordinary General Meeting (EGM) – these are now simply called 'general meetings'. They were any meeting of company members other than the annual general meeting.

extraordinary resolution – These no longer apply. Any resolution that was 'extraordinary' is now regarded as a 'special resolution'. A resolution required to effect decisions in certain circumstances (e.g. a creditors' winding-up) and which requires a majority of not less than 75 per cent of the company members voting in person or by proxy at a general meeting.

general meeting – a meeting of shareholders. It may be an Annual General Meeting or general meeting where shareholders give their approval for transactions.

incorporate – to form a limited company by following procedures prescribed by law. On incorporation the limited company becomes a separate legal entity distinct from its owners.

insolvency – the inability of a company to meet its debts as they become due.

issued shares – shares which have been actually allotted by the company and in respect of which the allottees have been entered in the company's register of members.

member – person whose name has been entered in the company's register of members in respect of the shares he holds in the company.

Memorandum of Association – the company's charter enabling the outsider to establish the extent of the company's powers.

minutes – written records of formal proceedings of shareholders' and directors' meetings.

Model Articles – regulations published by the government for the management of a company.

ordinary resolution – a decision reached by a simple majority (more than 50 per cent) of company members voting in person or by proxy.

poll – ascertaining the will of the shareholders at a general meeting of the company by counting shareholders' votes according to the size of their shareholdings.

pre–emption – the rights of existing shareholders granting them first option to acquire shares which are to be transferred or issued in proportion to their present shareholding.

proxy – authorisation by a shareholder allowing another to vote on his behalf.

Public Limited Company (PLC) – a type of company incorporated by registration under the Companies Act which may offer its shares to the public (a private company cannot do this) and is subject to a number of additional requirements under the Companies Act.

quorum – the number of shareholders or directors necessary for a vote in a valid meeting.

registered office – the postal address of the company notified to Companies House.

remuneration – payment for services.

resolution – decision made by directors or shareholders in accordance with requisite majorities set out in Articles of Association. Resolutions may be approved in meetings or by written resolution.

share certificate – written and executed instrument showing who holds title to a particular share or series of shares.

service business – a business that sells a service or advice instead of a tangible product.

shareholder – a holder of one or more shares in the capital of a company.

special resolution – a decision reached by not less than 75 per cent of company members voting in person or by proxy at a general meeting.

statutory books – the records that a company must keep as required by law. Changes must in many cases be notified to Companies House. The records should be kept at the company's registered office and be available to the public for inspection.

subscriber – a person who signs the Memorandum of Association and is issued the first shares in a new company.

Table A – for companies incorporated before 1 October 2009 these were the Model Articles. These have been replaced by Model Articles (see above).

written resolution – a resolution passed by either the shareholders or the directors of the company by signing a written form of the resolution rather than voting at a meeting of the company or at a meeting of the directors of the company.

Index

This index covers all chapters and the different types of forms in the Appendices.